SO YOU WANT TO SING BARBERSHOP

So You Want to Sing

Guides for Performers and Professionals

A Project of the National Association of Teachers of Singing

So You Want to Sing: Guides for Performers and Professionals is a series of works devoted to providing a complete survey of what it means to sing within a particular genre. Each contribution functions as a touchstone work not only for professional singers but also students and teachers of singing. Titles in the series offer a common set of topics so readers can navigate easily the various genres addressed in each volume. This series is produced under the direction of the National Association of Teachers of Singing, the leading professional organization devoted to the science and art of singing.

So You Want to Sing Music Theater: A Guide for Professionals, by Karen S. Hall, 2013

So You Want to Sing Rock 'n' Roll: A Guide for Professionals, by Matthew Edwards, 2014

So You Want to Sing Jazz: A Guide for Professionals, by Jan Shapiro, 2015

So You Want to Sing Country: A Guide for Performers, by Kelly K. Garner, 2016

So You Want to Sing Gospel: A Guide for Performers, by Trineice Robinson-Martin, 2016

So You Want to Sing Sacred Music: A Guide for Performers, edited by Matthew Hoch, 2017

So You Want to Sing Folk Music: A Guide for Performers, by Valerie Mindel, 2017

So You Want to Sing Barbershop: A Guide for Performers, by Diane M. Clark & Billy J. Biffle, 2017

SO YOU WANT TO SING BARBERSHOP

A Guide for Performers

Diane M. Clark
Billy J. Biffle

Allen Henderson
Executive Editor, NATS

Matthew Hoch
Series Editor

A Project of the National Association of
Teachers of Singing

ROWMAN & LITTLEFIELD
Lanham • Boulder • New York • London

Published by Rowman & Littlefield
A wholly owned subsidiary of The Rowman & Littlefield Publishing Group, Inc.
4501 Forbes Boulevard, Suite 200, Lanham, Maryland 20706
www.rowman.com

Unit A, Whitacre Mews, 26-34 Stannary Street, London SE11 4AB

Copyright © 2017 by Rowman & Littlefield

All rights reserved. No part of this book may be reproduced in any form or by any electronic or mechanical means, including information storage and retrieval systems, without written permission from the publisher, except by a reviewer who may quote passages in a review.

British Library Cataloguing in Publication Information Available

Library of Congress Cataloging-in-Publication Data

Names: Clark, Diane M. | Biffle, Billy J.
Title: So you want to sing barbershop : a guide for performers / Diane M. Clark, Billy J. Biffle.
Description: Lanham : Rowman & Littlefield, [2017] | Series: So you want to sing | "A Project of the National Association of Teachers of Singing." | Includes bibliographical references and index. | Description based on print version record and CIP data provided by publisher; resource not viewed.
Identifiers: LCCN 2017010198 (print) | LCCN 2017011581 (ebook) | ISBN 9781442266018 (electronic) | ISBN 9781442266001 (pbk. : alk. paper)
Subjects: LCSH: Barbershop singing—Instruction and study. | Barbershop quartets (Musical groups) | Barbershop quartets—History and criticism.
Classification: LCC MT875 (ebook) | LCC MT875 .C5 2017 (print) | DDC 783.1/4842—dc23 LC record available at https://lccn.loc.gov/2017010198

∞™ The paper used in this publication meets the minimum requirements of American National Standard for Information Sciences—Permanence of Paper for Printed Library Materials, ANSI/NISO Z39.48-1992.

Printed in the United States of America

To the Woolsocks men's ensemble of Rhodes College in Memphis, Tennessee, who in 1992 served as the catalyst for my entry into the fun and challenging world of barbershop singing, as well as to the many members of Sweet Adelines International and the Barbershop Harmony Society who have served as my mentors and teachers in this fascinating craft for the past twenty-five years. —Diane Clark

To Dr. Gregory K. Lyne and the late Jack Smith for their invaluable encouragement and mentorship in the early stages of my barbershop life; to the men of the Albuquerque Chapter of SPEBSQSA, Inc., who patiently supported me as I learned the craft; and to my many barbershop friends, who have supplied me with countless hours of joy, great music, and life-changing experiences over the past forty years. —Bill Biffle

CONTENTS

List of Figures ix

Series Editor's Foreword xi

Foreword by Tim Sharp xv

Acknowledgments xvii

Introduction: Who Sings Barbershop? xix

Online Supplement Note xxiii

1 The Barbershop Family Tree: A Brief History of Barbershop 1

2 Singing and Voice Science   *Scott McCoy* 13

3 Vocal Health for the Barbershop Singer   *Wendy LeBorgne* 31

4 The Barbershop Style: "Let's Bust a Chord!" 51

5 Barbershop Singing Technique: From Shower to Spotlight 67

6 Barbershop Ensembles: You Can't Do It Alone 81

7 Singing as One Voice: Techniques for Achieving Unit Sound 89

8 Standards for Barbershop Singing: Here Comes the Judge   103
9 Becoming a Better Barbershopper: Education in the Craft   111

Conclusion: The Barbershop Culture: Hobby or Lifestyle?   129

Glossary   133

Appendixes

   A: Resources   147

   B: How to Locate a Barbershop Chapter or Chorus   149

   C: International Quartet and Chorus Champions   153

   D: Choral Warm-ups—the Perfect Fifth—the Magic Interval
      Val Hicks   165

   E: Ten Steps to a Better Singing and Performing Chorus
      Greg Lyne   173

   F: How to Learn a Song   *Paula Davis, Carolyn Sexton, and
      Jay Giallombardo*   177

   G: Barbershop Humor   185

Index   191

About the Authors   205

FIGURES

Figure 1.1.	The Atlantic University Quartet	2
Figure 1.2.	The Bartlesville Barflies	5
Figure 1.3.	The Harmony Halls	6
Figure 1.4.	The Buffalo Bills	7
Figure 1.5.	The Suntones	8
Figure 1.6.	The Cracker Jills	10
Figure 2.1.	Location of diaphragm	15
Figure 2.2.	Intercostal and abdominal muscles	17
Figure 2.3.	External oblique and rectus abdominis muscles	18
Figure 2.4.	Layered structure of the vocal fold	20
Figure 2.5.	Cartilages of the larynx, viewed at an angle from the back	22
Figure 2.6.	Primary modes of vocal fold vibration	23
Figure 2.7.	Natural harmonic series, beginning at G2	24

Figure 2.8.	Typical range of first and second formants for primary vowels	26
Figure 4.1.	Major triad, barbershop-seventh chord, barbershop-ninth chord	54
Figure 4.2.	Major-sixth chord, major-seventh chord, major-ninth chord	55
Figure 4.3.	Minor triad, minor-sixth chord, minor-seventh chord	55
Figure 4.4.	Augmented triad, diminished-seventh chord	56
Figure 4.5.	Embellishment: Swipe	61
Figure 4.6.	Embellishment: Bell chord	61
Figure 4.7.	Embellishment: Post	63
Figure 6.1.	Voices Incorporated Chorus	83
Figure 6.2.	Fenton Lakes Chorus	87
Figure 8.1.	The Decaturettes	105
Figure 8.2.	For Heaven's Sake Quartet	109
Figure 9.1.	Open the Doors Youth Chorus	126

SERIES EDITOR'S FOREWORD

In the spring of 2000, I was completing my first year as a twenty-four-year-old high school choral director at Thomas A. Edison High School in Elmira Heights, New York, when I received an unexpected phone call. The kind and dignified gentleman on the other end of the line introduced himself as the president of the Mark Twain Barbershoppers—a local barbershop chorus that needed a choral director to prepare and coach them for their upcoming show. "What is a barbershop chorus?" I remember asking. I was about to find out!

That phone call quickly led to an "interview" over lunch at Manos Diner (across the street from the high school), where I was introduced to SPEBSQSA—which I was instructed to call "the Society" instead of trying to pronounce the acronym—heard stories about "the Salt Lake convention of 1980" and legendary quartets like the Boston Common, and was given a stack of barbershop CDs to go home and listen to. These men were clearly passionate about their hobby, and over the next eighteen months, I became immersed in the world of barbershop music, learning exactly why this genre is so special to so many people.

Weekly rehearsals became something of a ritual, just as much about the community and conversation over refreshment breaks as about the music. There was tireless dedication to tackling difficult music and singing as well as possible—perfectionism in the best sense of the word. These men and their wives became my good friends and possessed a generous spirit that I will never forget. A fun anecdote: as a first-year teacher, I was strapped for cash and owned an unreliable car that kept breaking down, but I never had to worry about getting a ride to work, a trip to the grocery store, or a jump start—all I had to do was call a barbershopper to help! My barbershop experience culminated in July of 2001 with a trip to Director's College at Harmony College, Western Missouri State College, in St. Joseph, Missouri, where I received conducting lessons from Jim Henry and Greg Lyne, heard the Gas House Gang perform, and met an enthusiastic young(ish) barbershopper named Bill Biffle, a man who would reenter my life fifteen years later as the coauthor of the book that you are reading right now.

Suffice to say, it was an absolute joy to reconnect with the world of barbershop by editing this volume. Diane Clark and Bill Biffle are a perfect pair of authors who bring a keen work ethic, dynamic working relationship, and rich perspectives as longtime barbershoppers. Diane, a retired professor of singing from Rhodes College in Memphis, deftly bridges the world between singing teachers and barbershoppers and also provides the reader insight into the "female" half of the hobby: Sweet Adelines International and Harmony, Incorporated. Bill brings over forty years of barbershop experience to these pages, having served the Barbershop Harmony Society as its president, as a certified master director and certified next level trainer, and as a faculty member at Harmony University, to name only a few of his many roles. His biography is accurate when it states that Bill "has done just about everything a barbershopper can do." Working with both of these individuals on this project was a deeply gratifying and enjoyable experience.

So You Want to Sing Barbershop: A Guide for Performers is the eighth book in the National Association of Teachers of Singing/Rowman & Littlefield So You Want to Sing series and the fifth book to fall under my editorship. Like other books in the series, there are several "common chapters" that are included across multiple titles. These include a chapter on voice science by Scott McCoy, as well as one on vocal health by Wendy LeBorgne. These chapters help to bind the series together, ensuring consistency of fact when it comes to the most essential matters of voice production.

SERIES EDITOR'S FOREWORD

The collected volumes of the So You Want to Sing series offer a valuable opportunity for performers and teachers of singing to explore new styles and important pedagogies. I am confident that voice specialists, both amateur and professional, will benefit from Diane M. Clark and Billy J. Biffle's important resource. It has been a privilege to work with both of them on this project. *So You Want to Sing Barbershop* is an invaluable resource for any performer or teacher who is interested in adding barbershop to their stylistic vocabulary.

Matthew Hoch

FOREWORD

One of the great opportunities I have in my role as executive director of the American Choral Directors Association is that of working with other organizations dedicated to inspiring excellence in vocal and choral music. Four of these vocal organizations are represented directly in *So You Want to Sing Barbershop*. These organizations are the National Association of Teachers of Singing (NATS), the Barbershop Harmony Society, Sweet Adelines International, and Harmony, Incorporated. As I work collaboratively with each of these organizations, I find we have three significant areas of overlap in our various goals and purposes:

1. We are passionately committed to inspiring people to sing.
2. We follow that commitment with the affirmation of the very best in vocal practice and hygiene.
3. We want people to enjoy singing throughout the full span of life.

In *So You Want to Sing Barbershop*, colleagues Diane M. Clark and Billy J. Biffle present an insightful, informative, instructive, intelligent, and readable introduction and discussion of the joy found in singing and particularly the joy of experiencing the wonderfully fulfilling vocal area of barbershop music. This book is for beginner and veteran, amateur and professional, student and teacher, and anyone interested in increasing their understanding of barbershop music and singing. NATS and Rowman & Littlefield continue to serve our profession significantly in this installment of the ongoing So You Want to Sing series.

Tim Sharp, Executive Director
American Choral Directors Association

ACKNOWLEDGMENTS

The authors express heartfelt gratitude to those friends and colleagues without whose contributions this book would never have come into existence.

First, we thank our series editor, Matthew Hoch, whose enthusiasm for the project and eye for detail helped to shape our efforts into an even more appealing package.

We thank the editors and staff at Rowman & Littlefield for their wise assistance: Natalie Mandziuk, Bennett Graff, Monica Savaglia, Kathleen O'Brien, and Lara Hahn.

We especially appreciate our expert readers and consultants: Kevin Keller, Christina Lewellen, Cynthia Linton, Lori Lyford, David Mills, Kim Vaughn, and David Wright.

We thank members of the National Association of Teachers of Singing (NATS): Allen Henderson, Jeannette LoVetri, and Matthew Edwards.

We thank members, staff, and friends of the Barbershop Harmony Society: Carlos Aguayo, Lillian Biffle, Al Bonney, Eric Dove, Jay Giallombardo, Chad Hall, Eddie Holt, Grady Kerr, Greg Lyne, Lorin May, Marty Monson, Don Rose, Paul Wietlisbach, and Todd Wilson.

We thank members and staff of Sweet Adelines International: Kelly Bailey, Holly Beck, Kay Bromert, Martha Clemons, Paula Davis,

Tamatha Goad, Richard Huenefeld, Nancy Leidel, Jeanne Lundberg, Vickie Maybury, Patsy Meiser, Emily Michael, Marcia Pinvidic, Renée Porzel, Carolyn Sexton, Lauren Stark, Tammy Talbot, Kay Todd, Melanie Trego, Kira Wagner, Kim Wonders, and Tena Wooldridge.

We thank members and staff of Harmony, Incorporated: Sandra Dalton, Jeanne O'Connor, Roxanne Powell, and Nicola Stevens.

Finally, we thank all the barbershoppers and NATS members who have cheered us on when they learned we were writing this book and who have expressed the desire to read it. We hope that it meets your high hopes and expectations.

INTRODUCTION

Who Sings Barbershop?

Welcome to the wonderful world of barbershop! Since you are reading this book, we know that you are interested in this exciting, challenging, life-changing American vocal style. The authors have devoted many years to the study and practice of this rewarding hobby and remain as eager as ever to sing it, teach it, and share it with you and others. There is much to learn, not the least of which are some vocal and ensemble skills that your previous studies and experience may not have provided you, but the culture—what barbershop is, who barbershoppers are, and what the future of barbershopping will almost certainly bring—is also important to become familiar with, if not to master, in this, your initial immersion in the style. Be assured that you will be welcomed, aided, and encouraged by barbershoppers everywhere as you take this journey. It's a family, the future is bright, there's room at the table, so come on in—the harmony is fine!

"Who sings barbershop?" you may ask. The answer is people of all descriptions. Barbershoppers, as we are affectionately known, are male, female, young, old, tall, short, fat, thin, American, non-American, amateur musicians, professional musicians, beginning singers, trained singers, NATS (National Association of Teachers of Singing) members, doctors, lawyers, homemakers, teachers, realtors, construction workers, truck drivers, retired persons, children, teenagers, parents, and grandparents. Barbershop singing is a G-rated, family-oriented, American art form. The requirements for singing barbershop are that you must be able to sing your part in English from memory, unaccompanied by instruments, and stay on your part while three other singers sing different harmony parts with you. You can do this in a chorus, where there are other singers also singing your part, or you can do it in a quartet, where you are the only one singing your part. And it helps if you can also perform simple choreography moves, although you will sometimes see singers in wheelchairs or special riser chairs or even accompanied by guide dogs on the performance stage. There is a place for everyone in the barbershop world. If you are not a singer, you can be a fan, a cheerleader, a supporter, a fund-raiser. You can sew costumes, build sets, prepare food. At our conventions, we often hear performances by a "family chorus," which is composed of barbershoppers who are related: siblings, cousins, aunts or uncles, nieces or nephews, children, parents, and grandparents. And the nonsinging family members are usually cheering wildly from the audience! We use the term *barbershop brat*, which refers to a barbershop singer who had one or two barbershop parents and grew up with barbershop in the home.

We, the authors, are pleased to introduce you to barbershop singing as part of the So You Want to Sing series, published by the National Association of Teachers of Singing and Rowman & Littlefield. This book seeks to introduce the barbershop art form to singers who have never sung it before and to vocal teachers who may want to know more about the genre in order to recommend it to their students or to assist their local barbershoppers with vocal skills. It also serves as a handbook for singers who have sung barbershop for many years. Barbershop singing originated as an art form for amateurs, and most barbershoppers today sing barbershop as a hobby, albeit one that demands time, hard work, skill, and a little money, as most hobbies do. People decide to sing barbershop for a great many reasons, and most who try it stick around for the long haul. In fact, almost every barbershopper will tell you, "I wish I had found barbershop sooner!"

Barbershop singers are active members of their communities, and barbershop choruses and quartets perform for all sorts of community events. Many groups will carol at holiday time or offer singing valentines or singing telegrams. Often choruses put on annual shows, which may also feature local and/or well-known quartets. Once or twice a year, most choruses and some quartets participate in regional competitions, where they are judged and scored according to an exacting set of standards that demand high-quality performances and demonstrable skill in the art form. Barbershoppers love their contests and are fully supportive of each other and of whoever wins. They respect each other and the achieving of excellence in the craft. They study the judges' comments to improve themselves for the next competition performance.

And after the performances are over, barbershoppers continue to sing. Groups of four or more often gather in a corner to sing tags, which are short segments of barbershop songs, usually the codas or embellished endings. Larger groups gather in hotel rooms, lobbies, or restaurants and pour their hearts out in song. Many performances have a cast party afterward—called in the culture an "afterglow"—where there is food and drink, and the singing goes on long into the night. Barbershoppers are happy people, full of joie de vivre, and they love to share their music with others.

We invite you to read this book and learn more about the great American art of barbershop singing. And we hope that you, too, will discover the life-enriching joys of this unique art form, as we have. ♪

ONLINE SUPPLEMENT NOTE

So You Want to Sing Barbershop features an online supplement courtesy of the National Association of Teachers of Singing. Visit the link below to discover additional exercises and examples, as well as links to recordings of the songs referenced in this book.

http://www.nats.org/So_You_Want_To_Sing_Book_Series.html

A musical note symbol ♪ in this book will mark every instance of corresponding online supplement material.

1

THE BARBERSHOP FAMILY TREE

A Brief History of Barbershop

THE BEGINNINGS

The beginnings of the vocal style we call *barbershop* are cloaked, as are those of most folk arts, in the mists of history. In the first few hundred years of the occupation of North America by Western Europeans and Africans brought over as slaves, these citizens of the "New World" looked, logically, to their ancestral homelands for their religion, art, music, crafts, and other elements of their culture. In the years before the American Civil War, this began to change. A new American culture—including a new kind of American music—appeared and began to grow. Since it was essentially a folk music form, this new music had predictable harmonies; simple, heartfelt lyrics; and melodies most amateurs could easily sing. And it was sung by most everyone. It was sung at home, in churches, on street corners, in the fields at work, on hayrides, around campfires, in army camps, in general stores, and—by male quartets—in places generally considered to be sole provinces of the men of the community, like drug stores and, yes, barbershops.

American composers—the most famous and prolific of whom was Stephen Foster (1826–1864)—wrote these simple folk-like songs for sale, and sell they did. Almost every home had a piano in the parlor and someone who could play it. As sheet music sales increased, singing together became a great American pastime. In addition to being accessible to most amateur singers, these songs were perfect for harmonizing in two, three, and even four parts. These, then, were the early characteristics of what came to be called *barbershop harmony*: simple, singable melodies; a chord on almost every melody note; the melody in the second-highest part; and heartfelt lyrics. These are the basic characteristics of the barbershop style we hear today. ♪

AFRICAN AMERICAN ROOTS

Every segment of America sang—amateur and professional, rich and poor, educated and uneducated, black and white—but it was probably the African American community that first created what we call the barbershop style. African American quartets on street corners, in barbershops, and in all kinds of public and private places were prevalent in the southern United States in the latter part of the nineteenth and the early

Figure 1.1. The Atlantic University Quartet. *Courtesy of the Barbershop Harmony Society*

THE BARBERSHOP FAMILY TREE

years of the twentieth centuries. Many famous African American musicians were connected with barbershop quartets. James Weldon Johnson (1871–1938), Scott Joplin (1868–1917), Jelly Roll Morton (1890–1941), Louis Armstrong (1901–1971), W. C. Handy (1873–1958), Sydney Bechet (1897–1959), and many others are known to have sung in quartets and to have promoted this type of harmony on stage, in barrooms, on street corners, and—for Scott Joplin's part—in an opera. This wonderful, spontaneous, freewheeling music, its roots intertwined with early blues and jazz, was an integral part of African American life in America. ♪

CROSSING THE CULTURAL DIVIDE

Sometime before the turn of the twentieth century, the music began to cross cultural barriers more rapidly. As it became increasingly popular in the ascendant parts of the culture, professional quartets began to record the music, vaudeville acts began to include quartets, and men began to come together in more formal foursomes at churches, fraternal organizations, city halls, fire stations, police departments, barbershops, and everywhere else that men gathered. By the early 1900s, quartets seemed to be everywhere. Then, with the advent of dance bands, radio, and other forms of entertainment that beckoned the participants to listen and dance but not to sing, this American style of four-part harmony began to decline. By the late 1930s, it was beginning to become a relic of a simpler, less hectic past—a thing to be remembered fondly, like hayrides, camp meetings, and quilting bees. Luckily for the many thousands of us whose lives have been enriched by singing this wonderful style, two men from Tulsa, Oklahoma, had a chance meeting in 1938, and the world of barbershop singing and that portion of the larger world that it touches haven't been the same since. ♪

SPEBSQSA, INC.

In the spring of that year, these two businessmen from Tulsa, Owen C. Cash (1892–1953) and Rupert Hall (1902–1972), found themselves marooned by a snowstorm at the Muehlebach Hotel in Kansas City. Falling into conversation, they soon discovered they both loved to harmonize. After a short search—the apocryphal story has it that they tipped a bellman to roam the lobby calling for a tenor and a bass—they found two other like-minded men and proceeded to sing their way deep into the night. Back home a few weeks later, buoyed by the experience, they invited fourteen men to convene on a rooftop at the Tulsa Club for a "songfest." While "quartetting" was their principal purpose, the group of twenty-six men who gathered that night sang together as a chorus, too. When singing the "old songs" together in four-part, close harmony proved to be a great success, they decided to meet again a week later.

The second meeting was moved to the Alvin Hotel, and when the windows were opened in response to the warm spring night, the hubbub caused a curious crowd to form outside. A passing wire-service reporter, sensing a story, wrote about it, and participating newspapers picked it up and spread it throughout the country. Much to the surprise of all, a vigorous movement in support of an international "barbershop harmony" organization soon appeared. After some gentle organizing by Cash, Hall, and a few others, the Society for the Propagation and Encouragement of Barber Shop Quartet Singing in America (SPEBSQSA)—a comedic attempt to parody the increasing quantity of New Deal organizations, with their lengthy names and resulting acronyms—was incorporated, and chapters began to spring up all over the continent. "Propagation" was later changed to "preservation" in the title, in hopes that the basic element of the style, the quartet, would live on, and the movement quickly spread.

The rapid growth of the Barbershop Harmony Society (BHS; trying to pronounce the acronym, SPEBSQSA, is impossible and strongly discouraged by the Society) was greatly aided by the existence of quartets in almost every town. When it became known that there was, in fact, an organization of "quartet singers" to join, men who loved this kind of harmony jumped on board at an astounding rate. By 1949, the Society had over twenty-six thousand members in 660 chapters in the United States and Canada. Rising to a peak of thirty-eight thousand members in 1983, today the organization boasts twenty-three thousand members in over eight hundred chapters in North America and has affiliates in nine foreign countries.

After the formation of SPEBSQSA, Inc., the style underwent some significant changes. The early quartets tended to be mainly comic performers. Fake handlebar mustaches, bizarre costumes, slapstick comedy, and general buffoonery marked the look and the programming of many of the earliest Society quartets. Appearances at local civic meetings, business openings, church and school functions, and the like were often in this vein—making fun, really, of the stereotypical quartets of old. In fact, the first Society champions, the Bartlesville Barflies, fit this image well when they won the first international championship in 1939. ♪

It didn't take long, however, with the advent of serious contests and frequent appearances by the better groups at important events and on radio and recordings, for more serious music making to take over. By the mid-1940s, excellent singers in polished ensembles became the model that quartets all over the continent strove to emulate. Typical of these were the Harmony Halls (1944 champions) in their white dinner jackets and black ties and—most importantly—the Buffalo Bills, champs in 1950. ♪

Certainly, one of the most important and influential quartets in the history of the style, this big-voiced quartet was an immediate hit on

Figure 1.2. The Bartlesville Barflies. *Courtesy of the Barbershop Harmony Society*

Figure 1.3. The Harmony Halls. *Courtesy of the Barbershop Harmony Society*

barbershop chapter shows all over the continent. After he heard one of their records, Meredith Willson invited the Buffalo Bills to audition for the part of the small-town school board in his new Broadway musical *The Music Man*. This produced a successful career for the quartet, as they appeared in 1,510 performances of the show on Broadway and in 1962 reprised their parts in the movie of the same name. Many appearances on radio and television, worldwide tours, concerts, conventions, and other appearances solidified their hold on the public's perception of the barbershop quartet for many years to come.

The next major change in the style was due, probably, to the acoustic properties of four voices singing together in tune, in synchrony, and with matching word sounds—namely, the "ring" of the barbershop sound. When good singers discovered how much fun it is to make that solid, exciting, almost visceral sound, they began to pursue it more intently, and by the mid-1950s or so, the "ring" had become the thing. Discovering that a bright, forward, "pingy" vocal sound produced high, audible overtones more easily, many quartets began to abandon the mellow, "studio" vocal tone for one that produced this powerful sound more

THE BARBERSHOP FAMILY TREE

Figure 1.4. The Buffalo Bills. *Courtesy of the Barbershop Harmony Society*

readily. Thus, for most of the 1960s, bright, forward singing was the norm. This "paint peeling" approach to the style was probably partially to blame for the style's poor reputation in the "legitimate" vocal world. Happily, though, this began to change rather quickly. Somewhere in the 1960s, professional quality vocalists singing with a smoother, more legato style, demonstrated that a high level of musicality and a more acceptable—at least to the "outside" world—vocal quality was possible while still producing the all-important "ring."

A small digression is needed here, for nestled in among the loud, high, ringy quartets of the 1960s—and continuing beyond the new emphasis on good-quality singing—was, arguably, one of the most influential barbershop quartets of all time, the 1961 champions, the Suntones. Composed of four professional-quality singers, this foursome sang together for over twenty-five years and always produced a vocally healthy, fully resonant, and entertaining sound that led to appearances on over one thousand chapter shows, a long run on the Jackie Gleason television show, and the production of ten record albums that remain popular with barbershop fans today. ♪

Figure 1.5. The Suntones. *Courtesy of the Barbershop Harmony Society*

The style has remained basically the same—everyone knows when a barbershop quartet is singing—throughout the rest of the twentieth century and, indeed, even to this day. There have been, of course, many talented and unique quartets who have had an outsized influence on the style, but the general barbershop sound remains much as it was in the 1970s—musical and vocally healthy when sung "right."

Barbershoppers all over North America met regularly to enjoy singing together. And, while singing in quartets was always the focus of these early meetings, group singing was a part of almost every get-together, too. It was inevitable, we suppose, for larger groups of barbershoppers to begin to sing together as a chorus for their family and friends. From this beginning, chorus singing—making, as it does, fewer demands on the singer to carry his part alone—gradually became the principal way men and women sing barbershop. Today, every chapter has a few quartets, but almost every member sings in the chorus at some level.

By 1953, choruses were included into the contest arena, too. The Great Lakes Chorus from Grand Rapids, Michigan, was crowned as the first-ever chorus champion from a field of sixteen. Over the intervening years, many great choruses have taken the stage in the Barbershop Harmony

Society, and some have dominated for a time. In fact, among them, three chapters—the Louisville Thoroughbreds, the Vocal Majority from Dallas, and the Masters of Harmony from Southern California—have won more than 43 percent of the contests held since the very beginning (twenty-seven of sixty-two). Currently, while many excellent barbershop choruses vie for supremacy each year, the Ambassadors of Harmony from the St. Louis area and the Westminster Chorus, also from Southern California, have proved to be the most consistent champions.

THE LADIES JOIN THE FUN: SWEET ADELINES INTERNATIONAL

By 1945, the ladies had had enough. Why were the men having all the fun? In the birthplace of SPEBSQSA—Tulsa, Oklahoma—a determined woman named Edna Mae Anderson called a meeting of a few wives of local barbershoppers, and from those beginnings the organization known as Sweet Adelines International (SAI) was born.

Keeping with tradition, the women sent invitations to all the wives of local barbershoppers, inviting them to meet at the Hotel Tulsa, the same place where the men first met to form their "club" in 1938. The response was overwhelming. By the end of the year, they were chartered in Oklahoma with eighty-five members and had a name, Atomaton, saluting the energy of the founding members and the dawn of the atomic age.

By the early 1950s, the organization, by that time known as Sweet Adelines, Inc., had grown to fifteen hundred members in twenty-five chapters in fourteen states, with all the trappings of a barbershop harmony organization—national officers, bylaws, and a contest system to choose the best quartet each year.

According to founder Edna Mae Anderson, "The original purpose for which Sweet Adelines was organized in 1945 was educational, to teach and train its members in musical harmony and appreciation," and the organization has remained true to this seminal intent. Today more than twenty-three thousand members sing in more than five hundred choruses and hold educational events and conventions all over the world, complete with hard-fought competitions for quartets and choruses alike.

Over the years, the ladies have sung the style in much the same manner as the men, working to produce a pleasing, in-tune, musically satisfying sound while creating as much barbershop "ring" as possible. While there have been dozens of excellent female quartets over the years, one, perhaps, stands out. In 1957, international champions—aka Queens of Harmony—the Cracker Jills immediately set a new standard for musicality, performance quality, and entertainment values. With four professional-quality singers; a big, bright, ringy sound; and a polished performer and prolific arranger, Renee Craig, singing lead, the quartet influenced the musical and performance style of the men's and women's organizations alike. ♪

Figure 1.6. The Cracker Jills. *Courtesy of Sweet Adelines International*

In 1973, the Sweet Adelines opened their competitions to choruses as well as quartets, and in the intervening years, some of the same names popped up on the gold medal list. The highest number of international chorus championships has been won by the Melodeers Chorus from Chicago, Illinois, and the Rich-Tone Chorus from Richardson, Texas, and the North Metro Chorus from Toronto, Canada, have both won several times. The first European chorus to win the international title was the Rönninge Show Chorus from Rönninge, Sweden, in 2013. The international Harmony Classic competition was begun in the year 2000, offering the opportunity for small and midsize choruses to compete against their peers.

HARMONY, INC.

In 1957, several members of Sweet Adelines, Inc., unhappy with what they perceived as a lack of representational government and with the group's adherence to a "whites only" membership (both BHS and SAI were limited to "whites only" until the mid-1960s), began to explore the possibility of forming another women's organization dedicated to the enjoyment of barbershop harmony singing. The new organization, Harmony, Inc. (HI), was founded in 1959. The approximately 150 original members were soon joined by other like-minded women, and the organization has continued to flourish today, with fifty-seven chapters, mostly in the eastern half of North America. According to HI's website, "while the two organizations (SAI and HI) continue to create wonderful music and friendships," HI's "musical focus mirrors the men's Barbershop Harmony Society in song selection, performance, and competition standards."

MIXED HARMONY

It's probable that there have always been barbershop ensembles that contained both males and females: a small-town chorus that needs a tenor, a barbershopper couple who want to sing with another barbershopper couple, a female quartet that needs a bass—possibilities abound. But in recent years, a movement to include mixed groups formally in the larger barbershop world has grown. There is, in fact, an organization dedicated to this form of barbershopping, appropriately called the Mixed Barbershop Harmony Association. According to their website, "The Mixed Barbershop Harmony Association (MBHA) is a not-for-profit charitable organization serving the needs of mixed barbershop harmony in North America. Established in 2016, its leadership comprises men and women with vast experience and participation in the barbershop style and performing in the mixed barbershop harmony genre. As of January 2016, the MBHA is an affiliate of the Barbershop Harmony Society." As of this printing, there are almost one thousand members of the Mixed Barbershop Singer Facebook page, and BinG! Barbershop in Germany, which is an organization for all barbershoppers, will hold the third World Mixed Harmony Competition in 2017, restricted to quartets with both male and female singers. ♪

AND NOW, THE WORLD!

Barbershop harmony is now sung all over the world. The oldest and largest organization outside of North America is the British Association of Barbershop Singers (BABS). Also active in England is the Ladies Association of British Barbershop Singers (LABBS), while other groups, male and female, thrive in Australia, China, Finland, Germany, Holland, Ireland, Japan, the Netherlands, New Zealand, Scotland, South Africa, Spain, Sweden, and the United Arab Emirates, among an ever-growing list. Both the BHS and SAI have had international champions, and representatives of affiliate organizations from all over the world appear each year at their international conventions, both as honored guests and as competitors. The two largest barbershop organizations are living up to their mottos, as the Barbershop Harmony Society aims to "keep the whole world singing!" while Sweet Adelines International wants to "harmonize the world!"

❷

SINGING AND VOICE SCIENCE

Scott McCoy

This chapter presents a concise overview of how the voice functions as a biomechanical, acoustic instrument. We will be dealing with elements of anatomy, physiology, acoustics, and resonance. But don't panic: the things you need to know are easily accessible, even if it has been many years since you last set foot in a science or math class!

All musical instruments, including the human voice, have at least four things in common, consisting of a power source, sound source (vibrator), resonator, and a system for articulation. In most cases, the person who plays the instrument provides power by pressing a key, plucking a string, or blowing into a horn. This power is used to set the sound source in motion, which creates vibrations in the air that we perceive as sound. Musical vibrators come in many forms, including strings, reeds, and human lips. The sound produced by the vibrator, however, needs a lot of help before it becomes beautiful music—we might think of it as raw material, like a lump of clay that a potter turns into a vase. Musical instruments use resonance to enhance and strengthen the sound of the vibrator, transforming it into sounds we identify as a piano, trumpet, or guitar. Finally, instruments must have a means of articulation to create the nuanced sounds of music. Let's see how these four elements are used to create the sounds of singing.

PULMONARY SYSTEM: THE POWER SOURCE OF YOUR VOICE

The human voice has a lot in common with a trumpet: both use flaps of tissue as a sound source, both use hollow tubes as resonators, and both rely on the respiratory (pulmonary) system for power. If you stop to think about it, you quickly realize why breathing is so important for singing. First and foremost, it keeps us alive through the exchange of blood gases—oxygen in, carbon dioxide out. But it also serves as the storage depot for the air we use to produce sound. Most singers rarely encounter situations in which these two functions are in conflict, but if you are required to sustain an extremely long phrase, you could find yourself in need of fresh oxygen before your lungs are totally empty.

Misconceptions about breathing for singing are rampant. Fortunately, most are easily dispelled. We must start with a brief foray into the world of physics in the guise of Boyle's Law. Some of you no doubt remember this principle: the pressure of a gas within a container changes inversely with changes of volume. If the quantity of a gas is constant and its container is made smaller, pressure rises. But if we make the container get bigger, pressure goes down. Boyle's Law explains everything that happens when we breathe, especially when we combine it with another physical law: nature abhors a vacuum. If one location has reduced pressure, air flows from an area of higher pressure to equalize the two, and vice versa. So if we can create a zone of reduced air pressure by expanding our lungs, air automatically flows in to restore balance. When air pressure in the lungs is increased, it has no choice but to flow outward.

As we all know, the air we breathe goes in and out of our lungs. Each lung contains millions and millions of tiny air sacs called alveoli, where gases are exchanged. The alveoli also function like ultra-miniature versions of the bladder for a bag pipe, storing the air that will be used to set the vocal folds into vibration. To get the air in and out of them, all we need to do is make the lungs larger for inhalation and smaller for exhalation. Always remember this relationship between cause and effect during breathing: we inhale because we make ourselves large; we exhale because we make ourselves smaller. Unfortunately, the lungs are organs, not muscles, and have no ability on their own to accomplish this feat. For this reason, your bodies came from the factory with special

SINGING AND VOICE SCIENCE

muscles designed to enlarge and compress your entire thorax (rib cage), while simultaneously moving your lungs. We can classify these muscles in two main categories: any muscle that has the ability to increase the volume capacity of the thorax serves an inspiratory function; any muscle that has the ability to decrease the volume capacity of the thorax serves an expiratory function.

Your largest muscle of inspiration is called the diaphragm (figure 2.1). This dome-shaped muscle originates from the bottom of your sternum (breastbone) and completely fills the area from that point around your ribs to your spine. It's the second-largest muscle in your body, but you probably have no conscious awareness of it or ability to directly control it. When we take a deep breath, the diaphragm

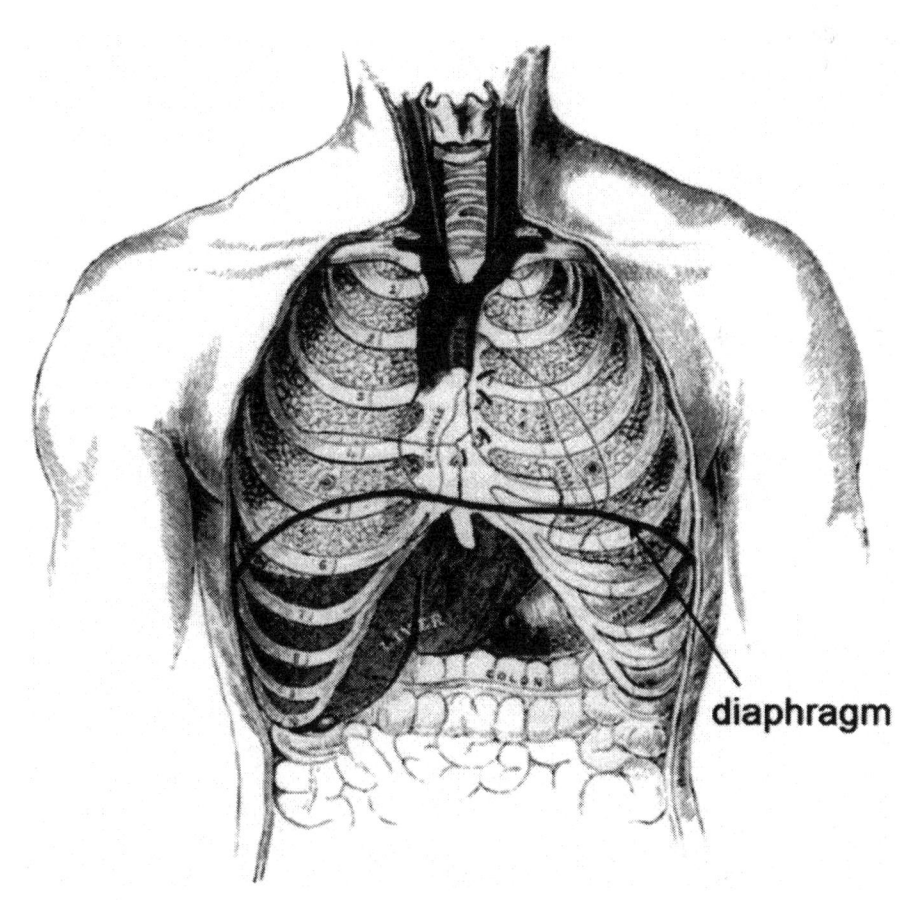

Figure 2.1. Location of diaphragm. *Courtesy of Scott McCoy*

contracts and the central portion flattens out and drops downward a couple inches into your abdomen, pressing against all of your internal organs. If you release tension from your abdominal muscles as you inhale, you will feel a gentle bulge in your upper or lower belly, or perhaps in your back, resulting from the displacement of your innards by the diaphragm. This is a good thing and can be used to let you know you have taken a good inhalation.

The diaphragm is important, but we must remember that it cannot function in isolation. After you inhale, it relaxes and gently returns to its resting position through an action called elastic recoil. This movement, however, is entirely passive and makes no significant contribution to generating the pressure required to sustain phonation. Therefore, it makes no sense at all to try to "sing from your diaphragm"—unless you intend to sing while you inhale, not exhale!

Eleven pairs of muscles assist the diaphragm in its inhalatory efforts, which are called the external intercostal muscles (figure 2.2). These muscles start from ribs one through eleven and connect at a slight angle downward to ribs two through twelve. When they contract, the entire thorax moves up and out, somewhat like moving a bucket handle. With the diaphragm and intercostals working together, you are able to increase the capacity of your lungs by about three to six liters, depending on your gender and overall physical stature; thus, we have quite a lot of air available to power our voices.

Eleven additional pairs of muscles are located directly under the external intercostals, which, not surprisingly, are called the internal intercostals (figure 2.2). These muscles start from ribs two through twelve and connect upward to ribs one through eleven. When they contract, they induce the opposite action of their external partners: the thorax is made smaller, inducing exhalation. Four additional pairs of expiratory muscles are located in the abdomen, beginning with the rectus (figure 2.2). The two rectus abdominis muscles run from your pubic bone to your sternum and are divided into four separate portions, called bellies of the muscle (lots of muscles have multiple bellies; it is coincidental that the bellies of the rectus are found in the location we colloquially refer to as our belly). Definition of these bellies results in the so-called ripped abdomen or six-pack of body builders and others who are especially fit.

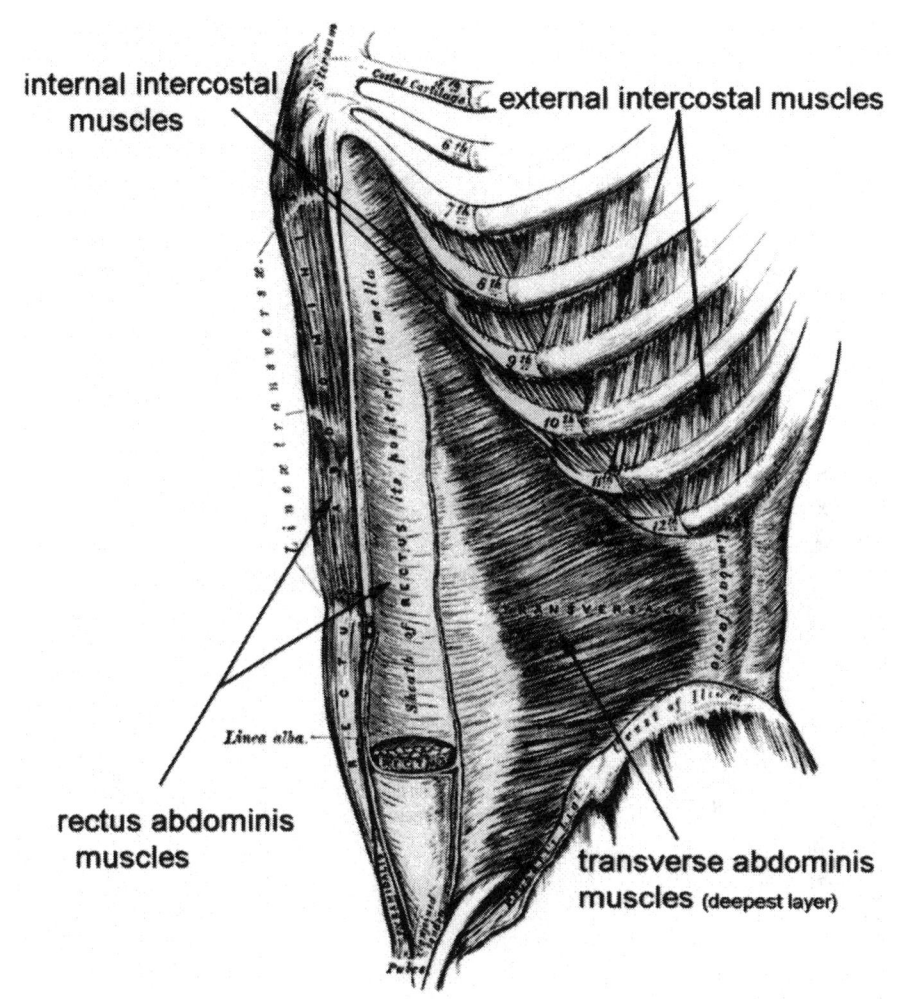

Figure 2.2. Intercostal and abdominal muscles. *Courtesy of Scott McCoy*

The largest muscles of the abdomen are called the external obliques (figure 2.3), which run at a downward angle from the sides of the rectus, covering the lower portion of the thorax, and extend all the way to the spine. The internal obliques lie immediately below, oriented at an angle that crisscrosses the external muscles. They are slightly smaller, beginning at the bottom of the thorax, rather than extending over it. The deepest muscle layer is the transverse abdominis (figure 2.2), which is oriented with fibers that run horizontally. These four muscle

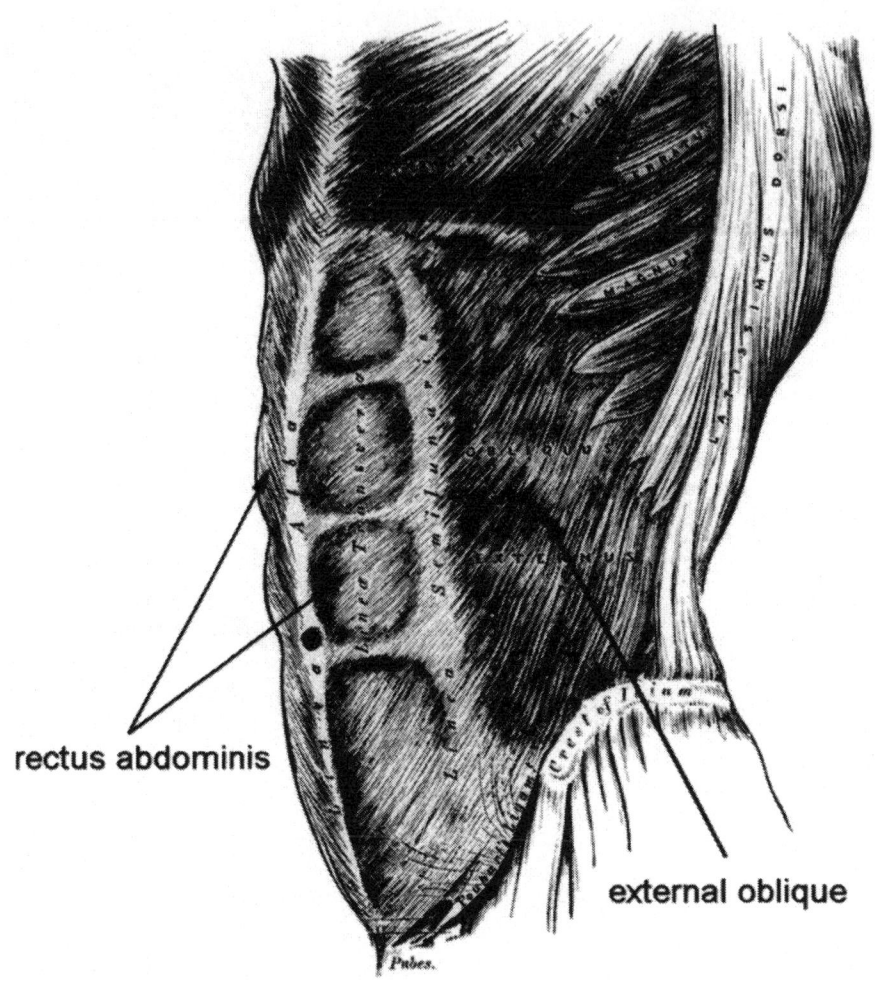

Figure 2.3. External oblique and rectus abdominis muscles. *Courtesy of Scott McCoy*

pairs completely encase the abdominal region, holding your organs and digestive system in place while simultaneously helping you breathe.

Your expiratory muscles are quite large and can produce a great deal of pulmonary or air pressure. In fact, they easily can overpower the larynx. Healthy adults generally can generate more than twice the pressure that is required to produce even the loudest sounds; therefore, singers must develop a system for moderating and controlling airflow and breath pressure. This practice goes by many names, including breath support, breath control, and breath management, all of which rely on the principle of muscular antagonism. Muscles are said to have an antagonistic relationship when they work in opposing directions, usually pulling on a common point of attachment, for the sake of increasing stability or motor control. You can see a clear example of muscular antagonism in the relationship between your biceps (flexors) and triceps (extensors) when you hold out your arm. In breathing for singing, we activate inspiratory muscles (e.g., diaphragm and external intercostals) during exhalation to help control respiratory pressure and the rate at which air is expelled from the lungs.

One of the things you will notice when watching a variety of singers is that they tend to breathe in many different ways. You might think that voice teachers and scientists, who have been teaching and studying singing for hundreds, if not thousands of years, would have come to agreement on the best possible breathing technique. But for many reasons, this is not the case. For one, different musical and vocal styles place varying demands on breathing. For another, humans have a huge variety of body types, sizes, and morphologies. A breathing strategy that is successful for a tall, slender woman might be completely ineffective in a short, robust man. Our bodies actually contain a large number of muscles beyond those we've already discussed that are capable of assisting with respiration. For an example, consider your latissimi dorsi muscles. These large muscles of the arm enable us to do pull-ups (or pull-downs, depending on which exercise you perform) at the fitness center. But because they wrap around a large portion of the thorax, they also exert an expiratory force. We have at least two dozen such muscles that have secondary respiratory functions, some for exhalation and some for inhalation. When we consider all these possibilities, it is no surprise at all that there are many ways to breathe that can produce beautiful singing. Just remember to practice some muscular antagonism—maintaining a degree of inhalation posture during exhalation—and you should do well.

LARYNX: THE VIBRATOR OF YOUR VOICE

The larynx, sometimes known as the voice box or Adam's apple, is a complex physiologic structure made of cartilage, muscle, and tissue. Biologically, it serves as a sphincter valve, closing off the airway to prevent foreign objects from entering the lungs. When firmly closed, it also is used to increase abdominal pressure to assist with lifting heavy objects, childbirth, and defecation. But if we gently close this valve while we exhale, tissue in the larynx begins to vibrate and produce the sounds that become speech and singing.

The human larynx is a remarkably small instrument, typically ranging from the size of a pecan to a walnut for women and men, respectively. Sound is produced at a location called the glottis, which is formed by two flaps of tissue called the vocal folds (aka vocal cords). In women, the glottis is about the size of a dime; in men, it can approach the diameter of a quarter. The two folds are always attached together at their front point but open in the shape of the letter V during normal breathing, an action called abduction. To phonate, we must close the V while we exhale, an action called adduction (just like the machines you use at the fitness center to exercise your thigh and chest muscles).

Phonation only is possible because of the unique multilayer structure of the vocal folds (figure 2.4). The core of each fold is formed by muscle, which is surrounded by a layer of gelatinous material called the lamina propria. The vocal ligament also runs through the lamina propria, which

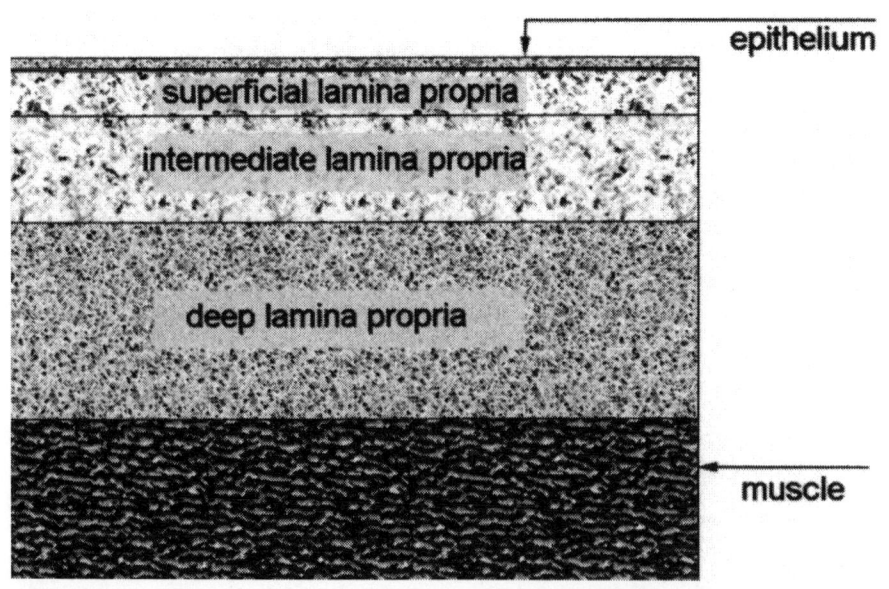

Figure 2.4. Layered structure of the vocal fold. *Courtesy of Scott McCoy*

helps to prevent injury by limiting how far the folds can be stretched for high pitches. A thin, hairless epithelial layer that is constantly kept moist with mucus secreted by the throat, larynx, and trachea surrounds all of this. During phonation, the outer layer of the fold glides independently over the inner layer in a wavelike motion, without which phonation is impossible.

We can use a simple demonstration to better understand the independence of the inner and outer portions of the folds. Explore the palm of your hand with your other index finger. Note that the skin is attached quite firmly to the flesh beneath it. If you poke at your palm, that flesh acts as padding, protecting the underlying bone. Now explore the back of your hand. You will observe that the skin is attached quite loosely—you easily can move it around with your finger. And if you poke at the back of your hand, it is likely to hurt; there is very little padding between the skin and your bones. Your vocal folds combine the best attributes of both sides of your hand. They provide sufficient padding to help reduce impact stress, while permitting the outer layer to slip like the skin on the back of your hand, enabling phonation to occur. When you are sick with laryngitis and lose your voice (a condition called aphonia), inflammation in the vocal folds couples the layers of the folds tightly together. The outer layer no longer can move independently over the inner, and phonation becomes difficult or impossible.

The vocal folds are located within the five cartilaginous structures of the larynx (figure 2.5). The largest is called the thyroid cartilage, which is shaped like a small shield. The thyroid connects to the cricoid cartilage below it, which is shaped like a signet ring—broad in the back and narrow in the front. Two cartilages that are shaped like squashed pyramids sit atop the cricoid, called the arytenoids. Each vocal fold runs from the thyroid cartilage in front to one of the arytenoids at the back. Finally, the epiglottis is located at the top of the larynx, flipping backward each time we swallow to prevent food and liquid from entering our lungs. Muscles connect between the various cartilages to open and close the glottis and to lengthen and shorten the vocal folds for ascending and descending pitch, respectively. Because they sometimes are used to identify vocal function, it is a good idea to know the names of the muscles that control the length of the folds. We've already mentioned that a muscle forms the core of each fold. Because it runs between the thyroid cartilage and an arytenoid, it is named the thyroarytenoid muscle

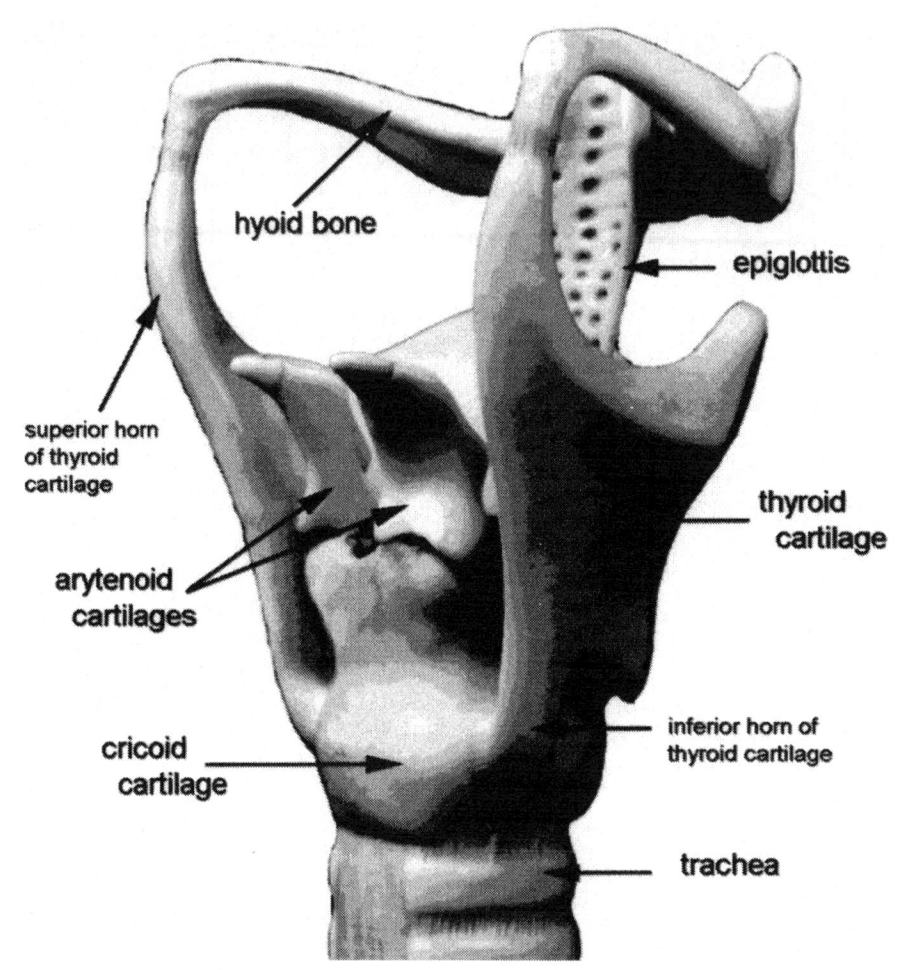

Figure 2.5. Cartilages of the larynx, viewed at an angle from the back.
Courtesy of Scott McCoy

(formerly known as the vocalis muscle). When the thyroarytenoid, or TA muscle, contracts, the fold is shortened and pitch goes down. The folds are elongated through the action of the cricothyroid, or CT muscles, which run from the thyroid to cricoid cartilage.

Vocal color (timbre) is created by the combined effects of the sound produced by the vocal folds and the resonance provided by the vocal tract. While these elements can never be completely separated, it is useful to consider the two primary modes of vocal fold vibration and their resulting sound qualities. The main differences are related to the relative thickness

SINGING AND VOICE SCIENCE

of the folds and their cross-sectional shape (figure 2.6). The first option depends on short, thick folds that come together with nearly square-shaped edges. Vibration in this configuration is given a variety of names, including Mode 1, thyroarytenoid (TA) dominant, chest mode, or modal voice. The alternate configuration uses longer, thinner folds that only make contact at their upper margins. Common names include Mode 2, cricothyroid (CT) dominant, falsetto mode, or loft voice. Singers vary the vibrational mode of the folds according to the quality of sound they wish to produce.

Before we move on to a discussion of resonance, we must consider the quality of the sound that is produced by the larynx. At the level of the glottis, we create a sound not unlike the annoying buzz of a duck call. That buzz, however, contains all the raw material we need to create speech and singing. Vocal or glottal sound is considered to be complex, meaning it consists of many simultaneously sounding frequencies (pitches). The lowest frequency within any tone is called the fundamental, which corresponds to its named pitch in the musical scale. Orchestras tune to a pitch called A-440, which means it has a frequency of 440 vibrations per second, or 440 Hertz (abbreviated Hz). Additional frequencies are included above the fundamental, which are called overtones. Overtones in the glottal sound are quieter than the fundamental. In voices, the overtones usually are whole number multiples of the fundamental, creating a pattern called the harmonic series (e.g., 100 Hz, 200 Hz, 300 Hz, 400 Hz, 500 Hz, etc. or G2, G3, D4, G4, B4—note that pitches are named by the international system in which the lowest C of the piano keyboard is C1; middle-C therefore becomes C4, the fourth C of the keyboard) (figure 2.7).

Glottis configuration
in mode 1 (chest voice)

Glottis configuration
in mode 2 (falsetto)

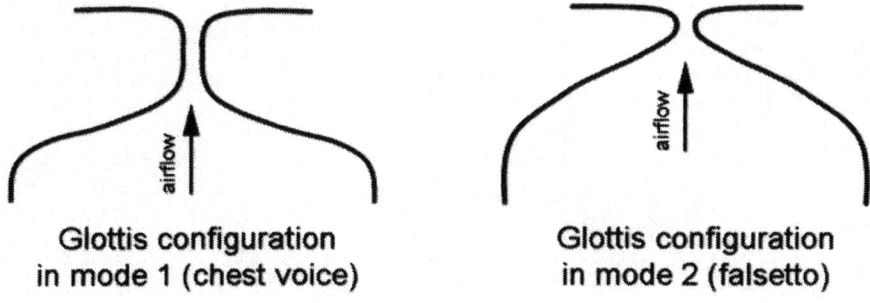

Figure 2.6. Primary modes of vocal fold vibration. *Courtesy of Scott McCoy*

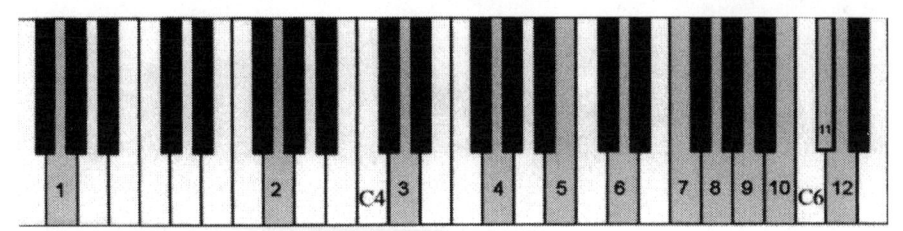

Figure 2.7. Natural harmonic series, beginning at G2. *Courtesy of Scott McCoy*

Singers who choose to make coarse or rough sounds as might be appropriate for rock or blues often add overtones that are inharmonic, or not part of the standard numerical sequence. Inharmonic overtones also are common in singers with damaged or pathological voices.

Under most circumstances, we are completely unaware of the presence of overtones—they simply contribute to the overall timbre of a voice. In some vocal styles, however, harmonics become a dominant feature. This is especially true in throat singing or overtone singing, as is found in places like Tuva. Throat singers tune their vocal tracts so precisely that single harmonics are highlighted within the harmonic spectrum as a separate, whistle-like tone. These singers sustain a low-pitched drone and then create a melody by moving from tone to tone within the natural harmonic series. You can learn to do this too. Sustain a comfortable pitch in your range and slowly morph between the vowels [i] and [u]. If you listen carefully, you will hear individual harmonics pop out of your sound.

The mode of vocal fold vibration has a strong impact on the overtones that are produced. In mode 1, high-frequency harmonics are relatively strong; in mode 2, they are much weaker. As a result, mode 1 tends to yield a much brighter, brassier sound.

VOCAL TRACT: YOUR SOURCE OF RESONANCE

Resonance typically is defined as the amplification and enhancement (or enrichment) of musical sound through supplemental vibration. What does this really mean? In layman's terms, we could say that resonance makes instruments louder and more beautiful by reinforcing the original vibrations of the sound source. This enhancement occurs in two primary ways, which are known as forced and free resonance (there is nothing pejorative in these terms: free resonance is not superior to forced resonance). Any object that is physically connected to a vibrator can serve as a forced resonator. For a piano, the resonator is the soundboard (on the underside of a grand or on the back of an upright); the vibrations of the strings are transmitted directly to the soundboard through a structure known as the bridge, which also is found on violins and guitars. Forced resonance also plays a role in voice production. Place your hand on your chest and say [a] at a low pitch. You almost certainly felt the vibrations of forced resonance. In singing, this might best be considered your private resonance; you can feel it and it might impact your self-perception of sound, but nobody else can hear it. To understand why this is true, imagine what a violin would sound like if it were encased in a thick layer of foam rubber. The vibrations of the string would be damped out, muting the instrument. Your skin, muscles, and other tissues do the same thing to the vibrations of your vocal folds.

By contrast, free resonance occurs when sound travels through a hollow space, such as the inside of a trumpet, an organ pipe, or your vocal tract, which consists of the pharynx (throat), oral cavity (mouth), and nasal cavity (nose). As sound travels through these regions, a complex pattern of echoes is created; every time sound encounters a change in the shape of the vocal tract, some of its energy is reflected backward, much like an echo in a canyon. If these echoes arrive back at the glottis at the precise moment a new pulse of sound is created, the two elements synchronize, resulting in a significant increase in intensity. All of this happens very quickly—remember that sound is traveling through your vocal tract at more than seven hundred miles per hour.

Whenever this synchronization of the vocal tract and sound source occurs, we say that the system is in resonance. The phenomenon occurs at specific frequencies (pitches), which can be varied by changing the position of the tongue, lips, jaw, palate, and larynx. These resonant frequencies, or areas in which strong amplification occurs, are called formants. Formants provide the specific amplification that changes the raw, buzzing sound produced by your vocal folds into speech and singing. The vocal tract is capable of producing many formants, which are labeled sequentially by ascending pitch. The first two, F1 and F2, are used to create vowels; higher formants contribute to the overall timbre and individual characteristics of a voice. In some singers, especially those who train to sing in opera, formants three through five are clustered together to form a super formant, eponymously called the singer's formant, which creates a ringing sound and enables a voice to be heard in a large theater without electronic amplification.

Formants are vitally important in singing, but they can be a bit intimidating to understand. An analogy that works really well for me is to think of formants like the wind. You cannot see the wind, but you know it is present when you see leaves rustling in a tree or feel a breeze on your face. Formants work in the same manner. They are completely invisible and directly inaudible. But just as we see the rustling leaf, we can hear, and perhaps even feel, the action of formants through how they change our sound. Try a little experiment. Sing an ascending scale beginning at B♭3, sustaining the vowel [i]. As you approach the D♮ or E♭ of the scale, you likely will feel (and hear) that your sound becomes a bit stronger and easier to produce. This occurs because the scale tone and formant are on the same pitch, providing additional amplification. If you change to a [u] vowel, you will feel the same thing at about the same place in the scale. If you sing to an [o] or [e] and continue up the scale, you'll feel a bloom in the sound somewhere around C5 (an octave above middle C); [a] is likely to come into its best focus at about G5.

To remember the approximate pitches of the first formants for the main vowels, [i]-[e]-[a]-[o]-[u], just think of a C-major triad in first inversion, open position, starting at E4: [i] = E4, [e] = C5, [a] = G5, [o] = C5, and [u] = E4 (figure 2.8). If your music theory isn't strong, you could use the mnemonic "every child gets candy eagerly." These pitches might vary by as much as a minor third higher and lower but no farther:

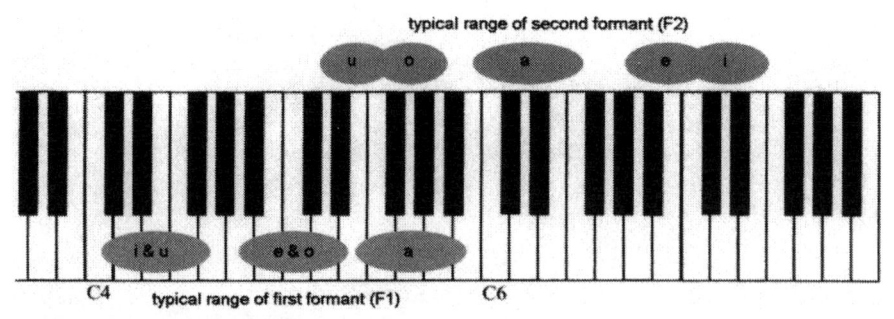

Figure 2.8. Typical range of first and second formants for primary vowels. Courtesy of Scott McCoy

once a formant changes by more than that interval, the vowel that is produced must change.

Formants have absolutely no preference for what they amplify—they are indiscriminate lovers, just as happy to bond with the first harmonic as the fifth. When men or women sing low pitches, there almost always will be at least one harmonic that comes close enough to a formant to produce a clear vowel sound. The same is not true for women with high voices, especially sopranos, who routinely must sing pitches that have a fundamental frequency higher than the first formant of many vowels. Imagine what happens if she must sing the phrase "and I'll leave you forever," with the word "leave" set on a very high, climactic note. The audience won't be able to tell if she is singing leave or love; the two will sound identical. This happens because the formant that is required to identify the vowel [i] is too far below the pitch being sung. Even if she tries to sing leave, the sound that comes out of her mouth will be heard as some variation of [a].

Fortunately, this kind of mismatch between formants and musical pitches rarely causes problems for anyone but opera singers, choir sopranos, and perhaps ingénues in classic music theater shows. Almost everyone else generally sings low enough in their respective voice ranges to produce easily identifiable vowels.

Second formants also can be important, but more so for opera singers than everyone else. They are much higher in pitch, tracking the pattern [u] = E5, [o] = G5, [a] = D6, [e] = B6, [i] = D7 (you can use the mnemonic "every good dad buys diapers" to remember these pitches) (figure 2.8). Because they can extend so high, into the top octave of the piano keyboard for [i], they interact primarily with higher tones in the natural harmonic series. Unless you are striving to produce the loudest unamplified sound possible, you probably never need to worry about the second formant; it will steadfastly do its job of helping to produce vowel sounds without any conscious thought or manipulation on your part.

If you are interested in discovering more about resonance and how it impacts your voice, you might want to install a spectrum analyzer on your computer. Free (or inexpensive) programs are readily available for download over the Internet that will work with either a PC or Mac computer. You don't need any specialized hardware—if you can use Skype or FaceTime, you already have everything you need. Once you've installed something, simply start playing with it. Experiment with your voice to see exactly how the analysis signal changes when you change the way your voice sounds. You'll be able to see how harmonics change in intensity as they interact with your formants. If you sing with vibrato, you'll see how consistently you produce your variations in pitch and amplitude. You'll even be able to see if your tone is excessively nasal for the kind of singing you want to do. Other programs are available that will help you improve your intonation (how well you sing in tune) or enhance your basic musicianship skills. Technology truly has advanced sufficiently to help us sing more beautifully.

MOUTH, LIPS, AND TONGUE: YOUR ARTICULATORS

The articulatory life of a singer is not easy, especially when compared to the demands placed on other musicians. Like a pianist or brass player, we must be able to produce the entire spectrum of musical articulation, including dynamic levels from hushed pianissimos to thunderous fortes, short notes, long notes, accents, crescendos, diminuendos, and so on. We produce most of these articulations the same way instrumentalists do, which is by varying our power supply. But singers have another layer of articulation that makes everything much more complicated; we must produce these musical gestures while simultaneously singing words.

As we learned in our brief examination of formants, altering the resonance characteristics of the vocal tract creates the vowel sounds of language. We do this by changing the position of our tongue, jaw, lips, and sometimes palate. Slowly say the vowel pattern [i]-[e]-[a]-[o]-[u]. Can you feel how your tongue moves in your mouth? For [i], it is high in the front and low in the back, but it takes the opposite position for [u]. Now slowly say the word Tuesday, noting all the places your tongue comes into contact with your teeth and palate and how it changes shape as you produce the vowels and diphthongs. There is a lot going on in there—no wonder it takes so long for babies to learn to speak!

Our articulatory anatomy is extraordinarily complex, in large part because our bodies use the same passageway for food, water, air, and sound. As a result, our tongue, larynx, throat, jaw, and palate are all interconnected with common physical and neurologic points of attachment. Our anatomical Union Station in this regard is a small structure called the hyoid bone. The hyoid is one of only three bones in your entire body that do not connect to other bones via a joint (the other two are your patellae, or kneecaps). This little bone is suspended below your jaw, freely floating up and down every time your swallow. It is a busy place, serving as the upper suspension point for the larynx, the connection for the root of the tongue, and the primary location of the muscles that open your mouth by dropping your jaw.

Good singing—in any genre—requires a high degree of independence in all these articulatory structures. Unfortunately, nature conspires against us to make this difficult to accomplish. From the time we were born, our bodies have relied on a reflex reaction to elevate the palate and raise the larynx each time we swallow. This action becomes habitual: palate goes up, larynx also lifts. But depending on the style of music we are singing, we might need to keep the larynx down while the palate goes up (opera and classical) or palate down with the larynx up (country and bluegrass). As we all know, habits can be very hard to change, which is one of the reasons that it can take a lot of study and practice to become an excellent singer. Understanding your body's natural reflexive habits can make some of this work a bit easier.

There is one more significant pitfall to the close proximity of all these articulators: tension in one area is easily passed along to another. If your jaw muscles are too tight while you sing, that hyperactivity will likely be transferred to the larynx and tongue—remember, they all are interconnected through the hyoid bone. It can be tricky to determine the primary offender in this kind of chain reaction of tension. A tight tongue could just as easily be making your jaw stiff, or an elevated, rigid larynx could make both tongue and jaw suffer.

Neurology complicates matters even further. You have sixteen muscles in your tongue, fourteen in your larynx, twenty-two in your throat and palate, and another sixteen that control your jaw. Many of these are very small and lie directly adjacent to each other, and you often are required to contract one quite strongly while its next-door neighbor must remain totally relaxed. Our brains need to develop laser-like control, sending signals at the right moment with the right intensity to the precise spot where they are needed. When we first start singing, these brain signals come more like a blast from a shotgun, spreading the neurologic impulse over a broad area to multiple muscles, not all of which are the intended target. Again, with practice and training, we learn to refine our control, enabling us to use only those muscles that will help, while disengaging those that would get in the way of our best singing.

FINAL THOUGHTS

This brief chapter has only scratched the surface of the huge field of voice science. To learn more, you might visit the websites of the National Association of Teachers of Singing (NATS), the Voice Foundation (TVF), or the National Center for Voice and Speech (NCVS). You can easily locate the appropriate addresses through any Internet search engine. Remember: knowledge is power. Occasionally, people are afraid that if they know more about the science of how they sing, they will become so analytical that all spontaneity will be lost or they will become paralyzed by too much information and thought. In my forty-plus years as a singer and teacher, I've never encountered somebody who actually suffered this fate. To the contrary, the more we know, the easier—and more joyful—singing becomes.

❸

VOCAL HEALTH FOR THE BARBERSHOP SINGER

Wendy LeBorgne

GENERAL PHYSICAL WELL-BEING

All singers, regardless of genre, should consider themselves as "vocal athletes." The physical, emotional, and performance demands necessary for optimal output require that the artist consider training and maintaining their instrument as an athlete trains for an event. With increased vocal and performance demands, it is unlikely that a vocal athlete will have an entire performing career completely injury free. This may not be the fault of the singer, as many injuries occur due to circumstances beyond the singer's control, such as singing through an illness or being on a new medication seemingly unrelated to the voice.

Vocal injury has often been considered taboo to talk about in the performing world, as it has been considered to be the result of faulty technique or poor vocal habits. In actuality, the majority of vocal injuries presenting in the elite performing population tend to be overuse and/ or acute injury. From a clinical perspective over the past seventeen years, younger, less experienced singers with fewer years of training (who tend to be quite talented) generally are the ones who present with issues related to technique or phonotrauma (nodules, edema, contact ulcers), while more mature singers with professional performing careers tend to present with acute injuries (hemorrhage) or overuse and misuse injuries (muscle tension dysphonia, edema, GERD) or injuries following an illness. There are no current studies documenting use and training in correlation to laryngeal pathologies. However, there are studies that document that somewhere between 35 percent and 100 percent of professional vocal athletes have abnormal vocal fold findings on stroboscopic evaluation. Many times these "abnormalities" are in singers who have no vocal complaints or symptoms of vocal problems. From a performance perspective, uniqueness in vocal quality often gets hired, and perhaps a slight aberration in the way a given larynx functions may become quite marketable. Regardless of what the vocal folds may look like, the most integral part of performance is that the singer must maintain agility, flexibility, stamina, power, and inherent beauty (genre appropriate) for their current level of performance, taking into account physical, vocal, and emotional demands.

Unlike sports medicine and the exercise physiology literature, where much is known about the types and nature of given sports injuries, there is no common parallel for the vocal athlete model. However, because the vocal athlete utilizes the body systems of alignment, respiration, phonation, and resonance with some similarities to physical athletes, a parallel protocol for vocal wellness may be implemented/considered for vocal athletes to maximize injury prevention knowledge for both the singer and teacher. This chapter aims to provide information on vocal wellness and injury prevention for the vocal athlete.

CONSIDERATIONS FOR WHOLE BODY WELLNESS

Nutrition

You have no doubt heard the saying "You are what you eat." Eating is a social and psychological event. For many people, food associations and eating have an emotional basis resulting in either overeating or being malnourished. Eating disorders in performers and body image issues may have major implications and consequences for the performer on both ends of the spectrum (obesity and anorexia). Singers should be encouraged to reprogram the brain and body to consider food as fuel. You want to use high-octane gas in your engine, as pouring water in your car's gas tank won't get you very far. Eating a poor diet or a diet that lacks appropriate nutritional value will have negative physical and vocal effects on the singer. Effects of poor dietary choices for the vocal athlete may result in physical and vocal effects ranging from fatigue to life-threatening disease over the course of a lifetime. Encouraging and engaging in healthy eating habits from a young age will potentially prevent long-term negative effects from poor nutritional choices. It is beyond the scope of this chapter to provide a complete overview of all the dietary guidelines for pediatrics, adolescents, adults, and the mature adult; however, a listing of additional references to help guide your food and beverage choices for making good nutritional choices can be found online at websites such as Dietary Guidelines for Americans, Nutrition .gov Guidelines for Tweens and Teens, and Fruits and Veggies Matter. See the online companion web page on the NATS website for links to these and other resources.

Hydration

"Sing wet, pee pale." This phrase was echoed in the studio of Van Lawrence regarding how his students would know if they were well hydrated. Generally, this rule of pale urine during your waking hours is a good indicator that you are well hydrated. Medications, vitamins, and certain foods may alter urine color despite adequate hydration. Due to the varying levels of physical and vocal activity of many performers, in order to maintain adequate oral hydration, the use of a hydration calculator based on activity level may be a better choice. These hydration calculators are easily accessible online and take into account the amount and level of activity the performer engages in on a daily basis. In a recent study of the vocal habits of musical theater performers, one of the findings indicated a significantly underhydrated group of performers.[1]

Laryngeal and pharyngeal dryness as well as "thick, sticky, mucus" are often complaints of singers. Combating these concerns and maintaining an adequate viscosity of mucus for performance has resulted in some research. As a reminder of laryngeal and swallowing anatomy, nothing that is swallowed (or gargled) goes over or touches the vocal folds directly (or one would choke). Therefore, nothing that a singer eats or drinks ever touches the vocal folds, and in order to adequately hydrate the mucous membranes of the vocal folds, one must consume enough fluids for the body to produce a thin mucus. Therefore, any "vocal" effects from swallowed products are limited to potential pharyngeal and oral changes, not the vocal folds themselves.

The effects of systemic hydration are well documented in the literature. There is evidence to suggest that adequate hydration will provide some protection of the laryngeal mucosal membranes when they are placed under increased collision forces as well as reducing the amount of effort (phonation threshold pressure) to produce voice. This is important for the singer because it means that with adequate hydration and consistency of mucus, the effort to produce voice is less and your vocal folds are better protected from injury. Imagine the friction and heat produced when two dry hands rub together and then what happens if you put lotion on your hands. The mechanisms in the larynx to provide appropriate mucus production are not fully understood, but there is enough evidence at this time to support oral hydration as a vital component of every singer's vocal health regime to maintain appropriate mucosal viscosity.

Although very rare, overhydration (hyperhidrosis) can result in dehydration and even illness or death. An overindulgence of fluids essentially makes the kidneys work "overtime" and flushes too much water out of the body. This excessive fluid loss in a rapid manner can be detrimental to the body.

In addition to drinking water to systemically monitor hydration, there are many nonregulated products on the market for performers that lay claim to improving the laryngeal environment (e.g., Entertainer's Secret, Throat Coat Tea, Greathers Pastilles, Slippery Elm, etc.). Although there may be little detriment in using these products, quantitative research documenting change in laryngeal mucosa is sparse. One study suggests that the use of Throat Coat when compared to a placebo treatment for pharyngitis did show a significant difference in decreasing the perception of sore throat.[2] Another study compared the use of Entertainer's Secret to two other nebulized agents and its effect on phonation threshold pressure (PTP).[3] There was no positive benefit in decreasing PTP with Entertainer's Secret.

Many singers use personal steam inhalers and/or room humidification to supplement oral hydration and aid in combating laryngeal dryness. There are several considerations for singers who choose to use external means of adding moisture to the air they breathe. Personal steam inhalers are portable and can often be used backstage or in the hotel room for the traveling performer. Typically, water is placed in the steamer and the face is placed over the steam for inhalation. Because the mucus membranes of the larynx are composed of a saltwater solution, one study looked at the use of nebulized saline in comparison to plain water and its potential effects on effort or ease to sound production in classically trained sopranos.[4] Data suggested that perceived effort to produce voice was less in the saline group than the plain water group. This indicated that the singers who used the saltwater solution reported less effort to sing after breathing in the saltwater than singers who used plain water. The researchers hypothesized that because the body's mucus is not plain water (rather it is a saltwater—think about your tears), when you use plain water for steam inhalation, it may actually draw the salt from your own saliva, resulting in a dehydrating effect.

In addition to personal steamers, other options for air humidification come in varying sizes of humidifiers from room size to whole house humidifiers. When choosing between a warm air or cool mist humidifier, considerations include both personal preference and needs. One of the primary reasons warm mist humidifiers are not recommended for young children is due to the risk of burns from the heating element. Both the warm mist and cool air humidifiers act similarly in adding moisture to the environmental air. External air humidification may be beneficial and provide a level of comfort for many singers. Regular cleaning of the humidifier is vital to prevent bacteria and mold buildup. Also, depending on the hardness of the water, it is important to avoid mineral buildup on the device and distilled water may be recommended for some humidifiers.

For traveling performers who often stay in hotels, fly on airplanes, or are generally exposed to other dry-air environments, there are products on the market designed to help minimize drying effects. One such device is called a Humidflyer, which is a face mask designed with a filter to recycle the moisture of a person's own breath and replenish moisture on each breath cycle.

For dry nasal passages or to clear sinuses, many singers use Neti pots. Many singers use this homeopathic flushing of the nasal passages regularly. Research supports the use of a Neti pot as a part of allergy relief and chronic rhinosinusitis control when utilized properly, sometimes in combination with medical management.[5] Conversely, long-term use of nasal irrigation (without taking intermittent breaks from daily use) may result in washing out the "good" mucus of the nasal passages, which naturally help to rid the nose of infections. A study presented at the 2009 American College of Allergy, Asthma and Immunology (ACAAI) annual scientific meeting reported that when a group of individuals who were using twice-daily nasal irrigation for one year discontinued using it, they had an increase in acute rhinosinusitis.[6]

Tea, Honey, and Gargle to Keep the Throat Healthy

Regarding the use of general teas (which many singers combine with honey or lemon), there is likely no harm in the use of decaffeinated tea (caffeine may cause systemic dryness). The warmth of the tea may provide a soothing sensation to the pharynx, and the act of swallowing can be relaxing for the muscles of the throat. Honey has shown promising results as an effective cough suppressant in the pediatric population.[7] The dose of honey given to the children in the study was two teaspoons. Gargling with salt or apple cider vinegar and water are also popular home remedies for many singers with the uses being from soothing the throat to curing reflux. Gargling plain water has been shown to be efficacious in reducing the risk of contracting upper respiratory infections. I suggest that when gargling, the singer only "bubble" the water with air and avoid engaging the vocal folds in sound production. Saltwater as a gargle has long been touted as a sore throat remedy and can be traced back to 2700 BCE in China for treating gum disease. The science behind a saltwater rinse for everything from oral hygiene to sore throat is that salt (sodium chloride) may act as a natural analgesic (pain killer) and may also kill bacteria. Similar to the effects that not enough salt in the water may have on drawing the salt out of the tissue in the steam inhalation, if you oversaturate the water solution with excess salt and gargle it, it may act to draw water out of the oral mucosa, thus reducing inflammation.

Another popular home remedy reported by singers is the use of apple cider vinegar to help with everything from acid reflux to sore throats. Dating back to 3300 BCE, apple cider vinegar was reported as a medicinal remedy, and it became popular in the 1970s as a weight loss diet cocktail. Popular media reports apple cider vinegar can improve conditions from acne and arthritis to nosebleeds and varicose veins. Specific efficacy data regarding the beneficial nature of apple cider vinegar for the purpose of sore throat, pharyngeal inflammation, and/or reflux have not been reported in the literature at this time. Of the peer-reviewed studies found in the literature, one discussed possible esophageal erosion and inconsistency of actual product in tablet form.[8] Therefore, at this time, strong evidence supporting the use of apple cider vinegar is not published.

Medications and the Voice

Medications (over the counter, prescription, and herbal) may have resultant drying effects on the body and often the laryngeal mucosa. General classes of drugs with potential drying effects include: antidepressants, antihypertensives, diuretics, ADD/ADHD medications, some oral acne medications, hormones, allergy drugs, and vitamin C in high doses. The National Center for Voice and Speech (NCVS) provides a listing of some common medications with potential voice side effects including laryngeal dryness. This listing does not take into account all medications, so singers should always ask their pharmacist about the potential side effects of a given medication. Due to the significant number of drugs on the market, it is safe to say that most pharmacists will not be acutely aware of "vocal side effects," but if dryness is listed as a potential side effect of the drug, you may assume that all body systems could be affected. Under no circumstances should you stop taking a prescribed medication without consulting your physician first. As every person has a different body chemistry and reaction to medication, just because a medication lists dryness as a potential side effect, it does not necessarily mean you will experience that side effect. Conversely, if you begin a new medication and notice physical or vocal changes that are unexpected, you should consult with your physician. Ultimately, the goal of medical management for any condition is to achieve the most benefits with the least side effects. Please see the companion page on the NATS website for a list of possible resources for the singer regarding prescription drugs and herbs.

In contrast to medications that tend to dry, there are medications formulated to increase saliva production or alter the viscosity of mucus.

Medically, these drugs are often used to treat patients who have had a loss of saliva production due to surgery or radiation. Mucolytic agents are used to thin secretions as needed. As a singer, if you feel that you need to use a mucolytic agent on a consistent basis, it may be worth considering getting to the root of the laryngeal dryness symptom and seeking a professional opinion from an otolaryngologist.

Reflux and the Voice

Gastroesophageal reflux (GERD) and/or laryngopharyngeal reflux (LPR) can have a devastating impact on the singer if not recognized and treated appropriately. Although GERD and LPR are related, they are considered as slightly different diseases. GERD (Latin root meaning "flowing back") is the reflux of digestive enzymes, acids, and other stomach contents into the esophagus (food pipe). If this backflow is propelled through the upper esophagus and into the throat (larynx and pharynx), it is referred to as LPR. It is not uncommon to have both GERD and LPR, but they can occur independently.

More frequently, people with GERD have decreased esophageal clearing. Esophagitis, or inflammation of the esophagus, is also associated with GERD. People with GERD often feel heartburn. LPR symptoms are often "silent" and do not include heartburn. Specific symptoms of LPR may include some or all of the following: lump in the throat sensation, feeling of constant need to clear the throat/postnasal drip, longer vocal warm-up time, quicker vocal fatigue, loss of high frequency range, worse voice in the morning, sore throat, and bitter/raw/brackish taste in the mouth. If you experience these symptoms on a regular basis, it is advised that you consider a medical consultation for your symptoms. Prolonged, untreated GERD or LPR can lead to permanent changes in both the esophagus and/or larynx. Untreated LPR also provides a laryngeal environment that is conducive for vocal fold lesions to occur as it inhibits normal healing mechanisms.

Treatments of LPR and GERD generally include both dietary and lifestyle modifications in addition to medical management. Some of the dietary recommendations include: elimination of caffeinated and carbonated beverages, smoking cessation, no alcohol use, and limiting tomatoes, acidic foods and drinks, and raw onions or peppers, to name a few. Also, avoidance of high-fat foods is recommended. From a lifestyle perspective, suggested changes include not eating within three hours of lying down, eating small meals frequently (instead of large meals), elevating the head of your bed, avoiding tight clothing around the belly, and not bending over or exercising too soon after you eat.

Reflux medications fall in three general categories: antacids, H2 blockers, and proton pump inhibitors (PPI). There are now combination drugs that include both an H2 blocker and proton pump inhibitor. Every medication has both associated risks and benefits, and singers should be aware of the possible benefits and side effects of the medications they take. In general terms, antacids (e.g., Tums, Mylanta, Gaviscon) neutralize stomach acid. H2 (histamine) blockers, such as Axid (nizatidine), Tagamet (cimetidine), Pepcid (famotidine), and Zantac (ranitidine), work to decrease acid production in the stomach by preventing histamine from triggering the H2 receptors to produce more acid. Then there are the PPIs: Nexium (esomeprazole), Prevacid (lansoprazole), Protonix (pantoprazole), AcipHex (rabeprazole), Prilosec (omeprazole), and Dexilant (dexlansoprazole). PPIs act as a last line of defense to decrease acid production by blocking the last step in gastric juice secretion. Some of the most recent drugs to combat GERD/LPR are combination drugs (e.g., Zegrid [sodium bicarbonate plus omeprazole]), which provide a short-acting response (sodium bicarbonate) and a long release (omeprazole). Because some singers prefer a holistic approach to reflux management, strict dietary and lifestyle compliance is recommended, and consultation with both your primary care physician and naturopath are warranted in that situation. Efficacy data on nonregulated herbs, vitamins, and supplements are limited, but some data do exist.

Physical Exercise

Vocal athletes, like other physical athletes, should consider how and what they do to maintain both cardiovascular fitness and muscular strength. In today's performance culture, it is rare that a performer stands still and sings, unless in a recital or choral setting. The range of physical activity can vary from light movement to high-intensity choreography with acrobatics. As performers are being required to increase their on-stage physical activity level from the operatic stage to the pop-star arena, overall physical fitness is imperative to avoid compromise in the vocal system. Breathlessness will result in compensation by the larynx, which is now attempting to regulate the air. Compensatory vocal behaviors over time may result in a change in vocal performance. The health benefits of both cardiovascular training and strength training are well documented for physical athletes but relatively rare in the literature for vocal performers.

Mental Wellness

Vocal performers must maintain a mental focus during performance and a mental toughness during auditioning and training. Rarely during vocal performance training programs is this important aspect of performance addressed, and it is often left to the individual performer to develop their own strategy or coping mechanism. Yet, many performers are on antianxiety or antidepressant drugs (which may be the direct result of performance-related issues). If the sports world is again used as a parallel for mental toughness, there are no elite-level athletes (and few junior-level athletes) who don't utilize the services of a performance/sports psychologist to maximize focus and performance. I recommend that performers consider the potential benefits of a performance psychologist to help maximize vocal performance. Several references that may be of interest to the singer include: Joanna Cazden's *Visualization for Singers* (Joanna Cazden, 1992) and Shirlee Emmons and Alma Thomas's *Power Performance for Singers: Transcending the Barriers* (Oxford, 1998).

Unlike instrumentalists, whose performance is dependent on accurate playing of an external musical instrument, the singer's instrument is uniquely intact and subject to the emotional confines of the brain and body in which it is housed. Musical performance anxiety (MPA) can be career threatening for all musicians, but perhaps the vocal athlete is more severely impacted. The majority of literature on MPA is dedicated to instrumentalists, but the basis of definition, performance effects, and treatment options can be considered for vocal athletes. Fear is a natural reaction to a stressful situation, and there is a fine line between emotional excitation and perceived threat (real or imagined). The job of a performer is to convey to an audience through vocal production, physical gestures, and facial expression a most heightened state of emotion. Otherwise, why would audience members pay top dollar to sit for two or three hours for a mundane experience? Not only is there the emotional conveyance of the performance but also the internal turmoil often experienced by the singers themselves in preparation for elite performance. It is well documented in the literature that even the most elite performers have experienced debilitating performance anxiety. MPA is defined on a continuum with anxiety levels ranging from low to high and has been reported to comprise four distinct components: affect, cognition, behavior, and physiology. Affect comprises feelings (e.g., doom, panic, anxiety). Affected cognition will result in altered levels of concentration, while the behavior component results in postural shifts, quivering, and trembling. Finally, physiologically the body's autonomic nervous system (ANS) will activate, resulting in the "fight or flight" response.

In recent years, researchers have been able to define two distinct neurological pathways for MPA. The first pathway happens quickly and without conscious input (ANS), resulting in the same fear stimulus as if a person were put into an emergent, life-threatening situation. In those situations, the brain releases adrenaline, resulting in physical changes of increased heart rate, increased respiration, shaking, pale skin, dilated pupils, slowed digestion, bladder relaxation, dry mouth, and dry eyes, all of which severely affect vocal performance. The second pathway that has been identified results in a conscious identification of the fear/threat and a much slower physiologic response. With the second neuromotor response, the performer has a chance to recognize the fear, process how to deal with the fear, and respond accordingly.

Treatment modalities to address MPA include psycho-behavioral therapy (including biofeedback) and drug therapies. Elite physical performance athletes have been shown to benefit from visualization techniques and psychological readiness training, yet within the performing arts community, stage fright may be considered a weakness or character flaw precluding readiness for professional performance. On the contrary, vocal athletes, like physical athletes, should mentally prepare themselves for optimal competition (auditions) and performance. Learning to convey emotion without eliciting an internal emotional response by the vocal athlete may take the skill of an experienced psychologist to help change ingrained neural pathways. Ultimately, control and understanding of MPA will enhance performance and prepare the vocal athlete for the most intense performance demands without vocal compromise.

VOCAL WELLNESS: INJURY PREVENTION

In order to prevent vocal injury and understand vocal wellness in the singer, general knowledge of common causes of voice disorders is imperative. One common cause of voice disorders is vocally abusive behaviors or misuse of the voice to include phonotraumatic behaviors such as yelling, screaming, loud talking, talking over noise, throat clearing, coughing, harsh sneezing, and boisterous laughing. Chronic or less than optimal vocal properties such as poor breathing techniques, inappropriate phonatory habits during conversational speech (glottal fry, hard glottal attacks), inapt pitch, loudness, rate of speech, and/or hyperfunctional laryngeal-area muscle tone may also negatively impact vocal function. Medically related etiologies, which also have the potential to impact vocal function, range from untreated chronic allergies and sinusitis to endocrine dysfunction and hormonal imbalance. Direct trauma, such as a blow to the neck or the risk of vocal fold damage during intubation, can impact optimal performance in vocal athletes depending on the nature and extent of the trauma. Finally, external irritants ranging from cigarette smoke to reflux directly impact the laryngeal mucosa and ultimately can lead to laryngeal pathology.

Vocal hygiene education and compliance may be one of the primary essential components for maintaining the voice throughout a career. This section will provide the singer with information on prevention of vocal injury. However, just like a professional sports athlete, it is unlikely that a professional vocal athlete will go through an entire career without some compromise in vocal function. This may be a common upper respiratory infection that creates vocal fold swelling for a short time, or it may be a "vocal accident" that is career threatening. Regardless, the knowledge of how to take care of your voice is essential for any vocal athlete.

Train Like an Athlete for Vocal Longevity

Performers seek instant gratification in performance sometimes at the cost of gradual vocal building for a lifetime of healthy singing. Historically, voice pedagogues required their students to perform vocalises exclusively for up to two years before beginning any song literature. Singers gradually built their voices by ingraining appropriate muscle memory and neuromotor patterns through development of aesthetically pleasing tones, onsets, breath management, and support. There was an intensive master-apprentice relationship and rigorous vocal guidelines to maintain a place within a given studio. Time off was taken if a vocal injury ensued or careers potentially were ended, and students were asked to leave a given singing studio if their voices were unable to withstand the rigors of training. Training vocal athletes today has evolved and appears driven to create a "product" quickly, perhaps at the expense of the longevity of the singer. Pop stars emerging well before puberty are doing international concert tours, yet many young artist programs in the classical arena do not consider singers for their programs until they are in their mid- to late twenties.

Each vocal genre presents with different standards and vocal demands. Therefore, the amount and degree of vocal training are varied. Some would argue that performing extensively without adequate vocal training and development is ill-advised, yet singers today are thrust onto the stage at very young ages. Dancers, instrumentalists, and physical athletes all spend many hours per day developing muscle strength, memory, and proper technique for their craft. The more advanced the artist or athlete, generally the more specific the training protocol becomes. Consideration of training vocal athletes in this same fashion is recommended. One would generally not begin a young, inexperienced singer on a Wagner aria without previous vocal training. Similarly, in nonclassical vocal music, there are easy, moderate, and difficult pieces to consider, pending level of vocal development and training.

Basic pedagogical training of alignment, breathing, voice production, and resonance are essential building blocks for development of good voice production. Muscle memory and development of appropriate muscle patterns happen slowly over time with appropriate repetitive practice. Doing too much, too soon for any athlete (physical or vocal) will result in an increased risk for injury. When the singer is being asked to do "vocal gymnastics," they must be sure to have a solid basis of strength and stamina in the appropriate muscle groups to perform consistently with minimal risk of injury.

Vocal Fitness Program

One generally does not get out of bed first thing in the morning and try to do a split. Yet many singers go directly into a practice session or audition without proper warm-up. Think of your larynx like your knee, made up of cartilages, ligaments, and muscles. Vocal health is dependent upon appropriate warm-ups (to get things moving), drills for technique, and then cool-downs (at the end of your day). Consider vocal warm-ups a "gentle stretch." Depending on the needs of the singer, warm-ups should include physical stretching; postural alignment self-checks; breathing exercises to promote rib cage, abdominal, and back expansion; vocal stretches (glides up to stretch the vocal folds and glides down to contract the vocal folds); articulatory stretches (yawning, facial stretches); and mental warm-ups (to provide focus for the task at hand). Vocalises, in my opinion, are designed as exercises to go beyond warm-ups and prepare the body and voice for the technical and vocal challenges of the music they sing. They are varied and address the technical level and genre of the singer to maximize performance and vocal growth. Cool-downs are a part of most athletes' workouts. However, singers often do not use cool-downs (physical, mental, and vocal) at the end of a performance. A recent study looked specifically at the benefits of vocal cool-downs in singers and found that singers who used a vocal cool-down had decreased effort to produce voice the next day.[9]

Systemic hydration as a means to keep the vocal folds adequately lubricated for the amount of impact and friction that they will undergo has been previously discussed in this chapter. Compliance with adequate oral hydration recommendations is important and subsequently so is the minimization of agents that could potentially dry the membranes (e.g., caffeine, medications, dry air). The body produces approximately two quarts of mucus per day. If not adequately hydrated, the mucus tends to be thick and sticky. Poor hydration is similar to not putting enough oil in the car engine. Frankly, if the gears do not work as well, there is increased friction and heat, and the engine is not efficient.

Speak Well, Sing Well

Optimize the speaking voice utilizing ideal frequency range, breath, intensity, rate, and resonance. Singers generally are vocally enthusiastic individuals who talk a lot and often talk loudly. During typical conversation, the average fundamental speaking frequency (times per second the vocal folds are impacting) for a male varies from 100 to 150 Hz and 180 to 230 Hz for women. Because of the delicate structure of the vocal folds and the importance of the layered microstructure vibrating efficiently and effectively to produce voice, vocal behaviors or outside factors that compromise the integrity of the vibration patterns of the vocal folds may be considered phonotrauma.

Phonotraumatic behaviors can include yelling, screaming, loud talking, harsh sneezing, and harsh laughing. Elimination of phonotraumatic behaviors is essential for good vocal health. The louder one speaks, the farther apart the vocal folds move from midline, the harder they impact, and the longer they stay closed. A tangible example would be to take your hands, move them only six inches apart, and clap as hard and as loudly as you can for ten seconds. Now, move your hands two feet apart and clap as hard, loudly, and quickly as possible for ten seconds. The farther apart your hands are, the more air you move and the louder the clap, and the skin on the hands becomes red and ultimately swollen (if you do it long enough and hard enough). This is what happens to the vocal folds with repeated impact at increased vocal intensities. The vocal folds are approximately 17 mm in length and vibrate at 220 times per second on A3, 440 on A4, 880 on A5, and more than 1,000 per second when singing a high C. That is a lot of impact for little muscles. Consider this fact when singing loudly or in a high tessitura for prolonged periods of time. It becomes easy to see why women are more prone than men to laryngeal impact injuries due to the frequency range of the voice alone.

In addition to the amount of cycles per second (cps) the vocal folds are impacting, singers need to be aware of their vocal intensity (volume). One should be aware of the volume of the speaking and singing voice and consider using a distance of three to five feet (about an arms-length distance) as a gauge for how loud to be in general conversation. Using cell phones and speaking on a Bluetooth device in a car generally result in greater vocal intensity than normal and singers are advised to minimize unnecessary use of these devices.

Singers should be encouraged to take "vocal naps" during their day. A vocal nap would be a short period of time (five minutes to an hour) of complete silence. Although the vocal folds are rarely completely still (because they move when you swallow and breathe), a vocal nap minimizes impact and vibration for a short window of time. A physical nap can also be refreshing for the singer mentally and physically.

Avoid Environmental Irritants: Alcohol, Smoking, Drugs

Arming singers with information on the actual effects of environmental irritants so that they can make informed choices on engaging in exposure to these potential toxins is essential. The glamour that continues to be associated with smoking, drinking, and drugs can be tempered with the deaths of popular stars such as Amy Winehouse and Cory Monteith who engaged in life-ending choices. There is extensive documentation about the long-term effects of toxic and carcinogenic substances, but here are a few key facts to consider when choosing whether to partake.

Alcohol, although it does not go over the vocal folds directly, does have a systemic drying effect. Due to the acidity in alcohol, it may increase the likelihood of reflux, resulting in hoarseness and other laryngeal pathologies. Consuming alcohol generally decreases one's inhibitions, and therefore you are more likely to sing and do things that you would not typically do under the influence of alcohol.

Beyond the carcinogens in nicotine and tobacco, the heat at which a cigarette burns is well above the boiling temperature of water (water boils at 212° F; cigarettes burn at over 1400°F). No one would consider pouring a pot of boiling water on their hand, and yet the burning temperature for a cigarette results in significant heat over the oral mucosa and vocal folds. The heat alone can create a deterioration in the lining, resulting in polypoid degeneration. Obviously, cigarette smoking has been well documented as a cause for laryngeal cancer.

Marijuana and other street drugs can cause permanent mucosal lining changes, depending on the drug used and the method of delivery. If you or one of your singer colleagues is experiencing a drug or alcohol problem, research or provide information and support on getting appropriate counseling and help.

SMART PRACTICE STRATEGIES FOR SKILL DEVELOPMENT AND VOICE CONSERVATION

Daily practice and drills for skill acquisition are an important part of any singer's training. However, overpracticing or inefficient practicing may be detrimental to the voice. Consider practice sessions of athletes:

they may practice four to eight hours per day broken into one- to two-hour training sessions with a period of rest and recovery in between sessions. Although we cannot parallel the sports model without adequate evidence in the vocal athlete, the premise of short, intense, focused practice sessions is logical for the singer. Similar to physical exercise, it is suggested that practice sessions do not have to be all "singing." Rather, structuring sessions so that one-third of the session is spent on warm-up; one-third on vocalises, text work, rhythms, character development, and so on; and one-third on repertoire will allow the singer to function in a more efficient vocal manner. Building the amount of time per practice session—increasing duration by five minutes per week, building to sixty to ninety minutes—may be effective (e.g., Week 1: twenty minutes three times per day; Week 2: twenty-five minutes three times per day, etc.).

Vary the "vocal workout" during your week. For example, if you do the same physical exercise in the same way day after day with the same intensity and pattern, you will likely experience repetitive strain–type injuries. However, cross-training or varying the type and level of exercise aids in injury prevention. So when planning your practice sessions for a given week (or rehearsal process for a given role), consider varying your vocal intensity, tessitura, and exercises to maximize your training sessions, building stamina, muscle memory, and skill acquisition. For example, one day you may spend more time on learning rhythms and translation and the next day you spend thirty minutes performing coloratura exercises to prepare for a specific role. Take one day a week off from vocal training and give your voice a break. This does not mean complete vocal rest (although some singers find this beneficial), but rather a day with no singing and limited talking.

Practice Your Mental Focus

Mental wellness and stress management are equally as important as vocal training for vocal athletes. Addressing any mental health issues is paramount to developing the vocal artist. This may include anything from daily mental exercises/meditation/focus to overcoming performance anxiety to more serious mental health issues/illness. Every person can benefit from improved focus and mental acuity.

VOCAL WELLNESS TIPS FOR BARBERSHOP SINGERS

The rehearsal structure for most barbershop choruses and quartets requires the singers to sing and/or coach for several hours at a time and then take a week or more off before singing again. The singers may or may not exercise their voices the rest of the week. A physical analogy can be made to this type of singing. If you only go to the gym and exercise for two hours two days a week, then you are more likely to fatigue and get injured then if you spread out your training and condition for a "longer (two-hour)" workout. Therefore, as a barbershop singer, try to sing for twenty to forty-five minutes daily to keep your voice conditioned and "in shape." On the flip side of the once-a-week rehearsals, as competitions approach, both the frequency and intensity of the rehearsals increase often resulting in vocal fatigue and occasionally vocal injury. Ensuring that the singers take "vocal naps" during the rehearsal process becomes challenging, especially when vocal blend and balance are at the core of barbershop singing.

Accurate intonation, vowel matching, and use of minimal vibrato to "lock in" a specific sound for a barbershop ensemble can result in undue vocal strain and tension if the singer is not adequately trained or vocally suited for this type of voice production for hours on end. Be sure at the end of each rehearsal (or as needed during the rehearsal), the singer reestablishes their vocal and physical neutral to allow for freedom of voice production.

Performance of barbershop music requires that the singer has a flexible, agile, dynamic instrument with appropriate stamina (in addition to a great ear for tight harmonies). The singer must have a good command of their instrument as well as exceptional underlying intention to what they are singing, as it is about relaying a message and connecting with the audience. The voices that convey barbershop music must reflect the mood and intent of the composer requiring dynamic control, vocal control/power, and an emotional connection to the text. They are often required to move or perform choreography while singing, which integrates physical as well as vocal flexibility.

FINAL THOUGHTS

Ultimately, the singer must learn to provide the most output with the least "cost" to the system. Taking care of the physical instrument through daily physical exercise, adequate nutrition and hydration, and focused attention on performance will provide a necessary basis for vocal health during performance. Small doses of high-intensity singing (or speaking) will limit impact stress on the vocal folds. Finally, attention to the mind, body, and voice will provide the singer with an awareness when something is wrong. This awareness and knowledge of when to rest or seek help will promote vocal well-being for the singer throughout his or her career.

NOTES

1. W. LeBorgne et al., "Prevalence of Vocal Pathology in Incoming Freshman Musical Theatre Majors: A 10-year Retrospective Study," Fall Voice Conference, New York, 2012.

2. J. Brinckmann et al., "Safety and Efficacy of a Traditional Herbal Medicine (Throat Coat) in Symptomatic Temporary Relief of Pain in Patients with Acute Pharyngitis: A Multicenter, Prospective, Randomized, Double-Blinded, Placebo-Controlled Study," *Journal of Alternative and Complementary Medicine* 9, no. 2 (2003): 285–298.

3. N. Roy et al., "An Evaluation of the Effects of Three Laryngeal Lubricants on Phonation Threshold Pressure (PTP)," *Journal of Voice* 17, no. 3 (2003): 331–342.

4. K. Tanner et al., "Nebulized Isotonic Saline versus Water Following a Laryngeal Desiccation Challenge in Classically Trained Sopranos," *Journal of Speech, Language, and Hearing Research* 53, no. 6 (2010): 1555–1566.

5. C. Brown and S. Graham, "Nasal Irrigations: Good or Bad?" *Current Opinion in Otolaryngology, Head and Neck Surgery* 12, no. 1 (2004): 9–13.

6. T. Nsouli, "Long-Term Use of Nasal Saline Irrigation: Harmful or Helpful?" American College of Allergy, Asthma and Immunology Annual Scientific Meeting, Abstract 32, 2009.

7. M. Shadkam et al. "A Comparison of the Effect of Honey, Dextromethorphan, and Diphenhydramine on Nightly Cough and Sleep Quality in Children and Their Parents," *Journal of Alternative and Complementary Medicine* 16, no. 7 (2010): 787–793.

8. L. Hill et al., "Esophageal Injury by Apple Cider Vinegar Tablets and Subsequent Evaluation of Products," *Journal of the American Dietetic Association* 105, no. 7 (2005): 1141–1144.

9. R. O. Gottliebson, "The Efficacy of Cool-Down Exercises in the Practice Regimen of Elite Singers," PhD dissertation, University of Cincinnati, 2011.

4

THE BARBERSHOP STYLE

"Let's Bust a Chord!"

In chapter 1 on the history of barbershop, we recounted the story of how people started to sing this uniquely American music. In this chapter, we want to take a closer look at just exactly what people are doing when they sing barbershop music. What makes it barbershop?

"LOCK AND RING": THE OVERTONES

In early days when amateur singers would get together and harmonize a simple song, they discovered that sometimes if they sang a certain way on certain chords, they could get a buzzing or ringing sound to occur, which was very satisfying to their ears. Over time, they were able to pinpoint the chords that most often produced this ringing sound, and eventually they came to understand the scientific principle behind the phenomenon. The chords that rang the best were the chords that reinforced the natural overtone series (as described by Scott McCoy in chapter 2). The simple songs they were singing were filled with three chords: the major triad (built on the first, fourth, or fifth steps of the major scale) and the dominant-seventh chord and dominant-ninth chord (both built on the fifth scale step). A fundamental pitch, plus the first five overtones of that pitch, were all reinforced by the major triad (e.g., F2, F3, C4, F4, A4, C5). That is, if a low voice sounded the fundamental pitch and other voices sang some of the upper pitches of that triad, tuned to match the frequencies in the overtone series, the overtones were reinforced, causing the chord to "ring." Happily, the sixth overtone in the series was the flatted seventh (E♭5 in the above example), which was reinforced by the dominant seventh chord—the chord that drives the harmony in most Western music (in this example, the F7 chord). The seventh overtone was again F (F6), and the eighth overtone was G (G6), which was reinforced by the dominant-ninth chord (the F9 chord). Since most early simple songs used mainly the tonic, dominant, and subdominant harmonies, which were the overtone-reinforcing chords, they lent themselves to the process of "ringing" chords.

The singers also found that if they could match their vowels more precisely, the chord would "lock" in and "ring" more easily. Thus "lock and ring" became the cornerstone of the barbershop sound. We often say that the main goal or purpose of barbershop singing is to "lock and ring" chords. When barbershop singers get together, this is what they want to do.

THE FOUR PARTS

Imagine some guys getting together to sing. One man takes the lead and sings the tune or melody of the song. Let's call him the lead. Three other men decide to harmonize with that melody. One man sings a low harmony; we'll call him the bass. Another man sings a higher harmony that lies above the melody; let's call him the tenor. And finally, we need someone to sing the missing note that fills out the chord. We will call him the baritone. If the melody goes high in range, then the baritone (bari for short) will sing a note below the melody—that is, between the lead and the bass parts. If the melody goes low, then the bari will sing a note above the lead—that is, between the lead and the tenor parts. Thus, the baritone part flip-flops around more than the others. Barbershoppers sometimes joke that the bari gets the leftovers or the notes that nobody else wants. Women's barbershop uses the same names for the four parts that the men use, so there are no sopranos or altos in barbershop, just as there are no first or second tenors among the men.

CHORD BALANCING

Because barbershop singing seeks to emphasize the tones that will cause chords to ring, proper chord balancing is one of the most important skills needed by barbershoppers. Typically, the bass voice strongly sounds the fundamental pitch, and the upper harmony parts sing more gently into the overtones of that fundamental. If the other parts sing their notes too strongly, they will be setting up new fundamentals with different series of overtones, and this will muddy the sound. To make chord balancing easier, a chorus may try to have a large-sized bass section, medium-sized lead and baritone sections, and a small tenor section. In a quartet, the chord balancing is totally the responsibility of the individual singers. This need for strength in the bass part is one reason that barbershop is sometimes described as a "bass-driven art form."

VOWEL MATCHING AND SYNCHRONIZATION

It is not uncommon for choral groups of various genres to aim for matching vowels to enhance resonance. However, this challenge is especially important in barbershop singing:

> Use of similar word sounds in good quality and optimum volume relationships by each of the voice parts further enhances the sensation of consonance by mutual reinforcement of the harmonics (overtones) to produce the unique full or "expanded" sound characteristic of barbershop harmony.[1]

Because barbershop is an American art form, most of our songs are sung in Standard American English. Of course, it is fun and often moving when we hear our international members sing songs that have been arranged in the barbershop style in their native languages, but in American barbershop competitions, songs in English are the norm. Since Standard American English is more of a model language (like *Hochdeutsch* or "High" German) and not spoken by many people, except perhaps voice professionals, it is a great challenge for barbershop singers to overcome their regional dialects and mold their sounds into a unit that can "lock and ring."

In addition to matching their vowels, barbershop singers must learn to sing cleanly and with precision so that all the word and pitch sounds are carefully synchronized. Scooping up to pitches, chewing or closing off vowels, sustaining consonants, and other such stylizations that are highly valued in much pop-style music are not encouraged in barbershop singing, because these imprecise habits tend to impede the "lock and ring."

THE ELEVEN CHORDS

Barbershop music is homophonic or "chordal" in style. There is a melody that is harmonized by three other voices. There is traditionally no polyphony (multiple independent melodies) in barbershop. Voice leading is kept as smooth as possible; in other words, each part moves from note to note as efficiently as can be arranged. However, keeping the root and the fifth of the chords in the lowest parts (bass and baritone) to achieve the maximum "ring" often leads to what others might call violations of part-writing rules.[2] Parallel fifths, for example, occur fairly often in barbershop music due to the desire to keep the bass and baritone on these important pitches.

Many musicians are surprised to learn that barbershop music mainly uses eleven chords. Often they say, "Well, isn't that boring?" But this comment just shows that they are unaware of the purpose of barbershop, which is to lock and ring chords by reinforcing the natural overtones. Not only does barbershop music mainly use eleven chords, but it primarily uses the "big three"—the major triad, the dominant seventh, and the dominant ninth.

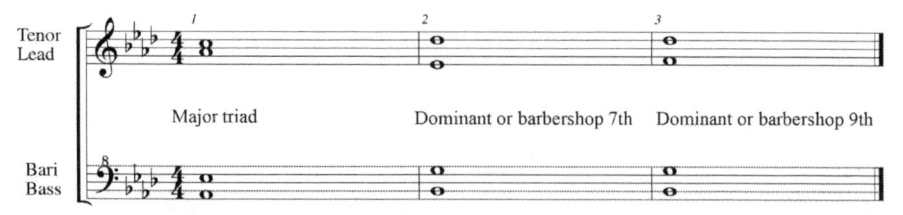

Figure 4.1. Major triad, barbershop-seventh chord, barbershop-ninth chord. *Courtesy of the authors*

THE BARBERSHOP STYLE

In fact, these latter two chords are so important to the barbershop sound that we even call them the "barbershop seventh" and the "barbershop ninth." These three main chords are considered strong chords because they provide the best chance for achieving lock and ring by reinforcing the overtones. These three chords are used as much as possible in a strong barbershop arrangement, and they are typically used at all strong points within the song—for example, strong beats, beginnings of sections, cadences, and key changes.

Eight additional chords are used primarily for color and variety. These color chords are:

major-sixth chord
major-seventh chord
major-ninth chord

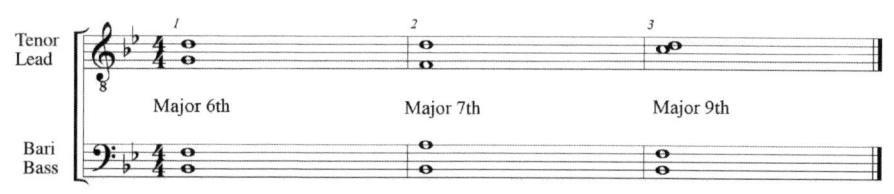

Figure 4.2. Major-sixth chord, major-seventh chord, major-ninth chord. *Courtesy of the authors*

minor triad
minor-sixth chord
minor-seventh chord

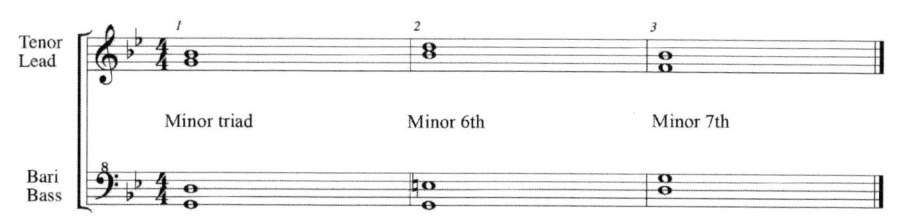

Figure 4.3. Minor triad, minor-sixth chord, minor-seventh chord. *Courtesy of the authors*

augmented triad
diminished-seventh chord

```
Tenor    1                    2
Lead    o                     o
        #o                    #o
        Augmented triad       Diminished 7th
        o                     o
Bari
Bass    o                     #o
```

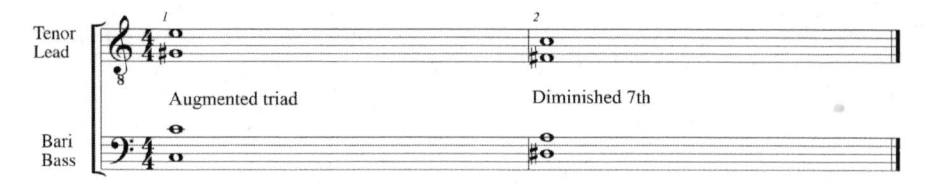

Figure 4.4. Augmented triad, diminished-seventh chord. *Courtesy of the authors*

Almost any song can be arranged in the barbershop style or format, and barbershoppers enjoy variety as much as anyone else, so we perform jazz songs and show tunes and songs from other musical genres that we arrange to suit our particular four-part format. Notable barbershop arranger Kevin Keller states: "Barbershop definitely has defining characteristics and that should be captured. However, it is an art form that not only evolves, but is exploratory in its very essence. Barbershoppers are constantly trying to find new and inventive ways to sing barbershop, both in style as well as delivery and presentation."[3] But in the end, a barbershop arranger has one main goal, and that is to build into the music arrangement itself more opportunities for the singers to ring chords.

TUNING

The piano is tuned or tempered so that each of the twelve tones of the chromatic scale are the same distance apart.[4] The pianist has no responsibility for tuning; he simply strikes the key to make the sound. Other instruments can adjust their tuning so that a pitch can be slightly higher or lower, according to the pitch's function in the scale or the chord. A violinist, for example, may choose to play D♯ slightly higher than its enharmonic equivalent E♭. Barbershoppers work to sing intuitively with this kind of pitch adjustment, since this tuning corresponds inherently with the frequencies of the overtone series, causing the overtones to ring more easily.

The Barbershop Harmony Society's *Barbershop Arranging Manual* includes this statement about tuning in its definition of barbershop harmony:

> Relative to an established sense of tonality, the melody line and the harmony parts are enharmonically adjusted in pitch to produce an optimum

consonant sound. The resulting pitch relationships are often considerably at variance with those defined by the equal temperament of fixed-pitch instruments.[5] ♪

THE SHEET MUSIC (AKA THE CHART)

Modern barbershoppers take pride in their ability to read music, regardless of whether they are amateur or professional musicians. Even beginners are encouraged to learn more about what they see on the page. So let's take a look at what a barbershop chart looks like.

Barbershop music is generally sung a cappella (unaccompanied by instruments), and the music is written on the grand staff. The upper staff uses the treble clef and contains the melody of the song (the lead part) and a part that sings a harmony above the melody (the tenor part). In men's music, the treble clef may have a tiny "8" at the bottom, showing that the tenor and lead parts are to be sung an octave lower than written. The lower staff uses the bass clef, and the parts located here are the baritone (upper) and the bass (lower). In women's barbershop music, the bass clef may have a tiny "8" on top, indicating that the baritones and basses should sing their parts an octave higher than written.

As we mentioned earlier, most barbershop songs are sung in English. Since most of the time all four parts are singing the same words, the words are normally positioned in between the two staves, just below the lead or melody part. When the harmony parts sing different words, their words are written as close to the part as possible—tenor and baritone above their respective staves, and bass below.

Most barbershop songs are popular songs in the style of the Great American Songbook, made popular by such composers as Irving Berlin, George Gershwin, Jerome Kern, Cole Porter, and Richard Rodgers. Some variations of this form are AABA, ABAB, ABAC, or ABCA. This form is generally found in the chorus of the song, which typically contains thirty-two measures—hence the common reference to "32-bar song form." The song may have a verse, often of sixteen measures. Sometimes the verse will serve as the introduction to the song, but frequently an arranger will create an introduction (intro) of four or eight measures to set up the song. And almost every barbershop song ends with a tag, which is like a coda in classical music. It is an embellishment that brings the song to a dramatic finish. Tags are so important in barbershop singing that they are often excerpted from their original songs and sung as stand-alone numbers. And there are tags written that were never a part of any song but simply give the singers more opportunities to have fun ringing chords.

When looking at a barbershop chart, it is usually obvious whether it is a men's arrangement or a women's arrangement. In the men's charts, the voice parts are spread out more widely, whereas the women's charts use a more closely voiced arrangement. Simplistically, it has been said that men's voices naturally have depth, so their arrangements seek to add brilliance, whereas women's voices naturally have brilliance, so their arrangements seek to add depth. In truth, the difference in the way the parts are positioned has to do with the physics of sound, since "lock and ring" is more easily achieved at higher frequencies with tighter voicings.[6] The men also sing in different keys from the women, so as to make use of the most comfortable ranges for all voices. Depending on whether the melody spans *do* to *do* (first scale step) or *sol* to *sol* (fifth scale step), the most common keys for the men are B♭ and F, whereas the women most often use A♭ and E♭.

Barbershop songs written in the major mode obviously enhance "lock and ring" potential. According to Keller, songs that are in minor keys "actually make great barbershop vehicles,"[7] though they may present some challenges to the achieving of "lock and ring." Songs in minor keys are sometimes ended with a major third (this device is called a Picardy third) to maximize "ring" potential.

RHYTHM AND TEMPO: BALLAD, UPTUNE, AND SWING TUNE

The two traditional types of barbershop songs are uptunes and ballads, or fast songs and slow songs. A third very popular type of barbershop song is the swing tune, which can be fast or slow. The key to each is the element of rhythm.

An uptune has the musical rhythm as its driving force. The song is generally sung at a fast tempo, and the rhythm is steady enough for the

THE BARBERSHOP STYLE

audience to tap their feet to it. Occasionally, there may be some temporary alteration from this driving rhythmic pattern, such as a "stomp" section sung at half-tempo or a grand slowing down (ritardando) at the end, but the majority of the song moves forward steadily with a consistent, regular beat and with emphasis on the strong beats (e.g., beats 1 and 3 in 4/4 meter). Barbershop music generally makes use of regular rhythmic meters such as 4/4, 3/4, 2/2, and 6/8. Irregular meters such as 5/8 or 7/8 are typically not used. ♪

The barbershop ballad is one of the unique aspects of the barbershop style. The rhythm of a barbershop ballad is almost completely text driven. The singers offer up the text almost as though they are speaking it, telling a wonderful story full of passion and emotion. Ballads are exciting to sing and thrilling to hear. They tug at the heartstrings. Often trained classical musicians are distressed when they first come to a barbershop rehearsal and discover that a half note may not really get two beats. In a barbershop ballad, no one is concerned about half notes getting two beats. The important thing is delivering the message of the words in a meaningful way. The half-note indication may tell us something about the relative importance of one word over another, but no one will be counting beats in a barbershop ballad. Ballad singing is one of the highlights of barbershop music, and it is a great challenge to interpret and perform ballads effectively. ♪

The swing tune is a third type of song that is popular with barbershoppers. Musical rhythm is the strong element of the swing tune. In 4/4 meter, the double-eighth-note rhythm is performed as a quarter- and eighth-note triplet. Occasionally, a pair of eighth notes are written as a dotted eighth and a sixteenth note, but this only approximates the "swing" nature of a pair of eighth notes. Swing tunes emphasize the "backbeat"—that is, beats 2 and 4 in a 4/4 meter. ♪

EMBELLISHMENTS

Because barbershop music is generally sung a cappella, there is no instrumental accompaniment to provide rhythmic movement for the song. All forward motion must be created by the singers themselves. This is easier in an uptune or swing tune, where the musical rhythm is the driving force, but it can be harder in a ballad, which will have some longer, held notes. Thus, barbershop music uses various devices called embellishments, which encourage forward motion and give the singers a chance to express more emotion at a particular spot. Nancy Bergman defines an embellishment as "any musical notation beyond the vertical chording of the melody line."[8] According to Dale Syverson, "Embellishments represent points of emphasis or heightened emotion within your phrasing plan. Use them to help you build momentum toward the climax of the song."[9]

Any barbershop arrangement can be expected to contain several of the following embellishments:

- *Tag*—We have already mentioned the tag or ending of the song. This is a four to eight-measure elaboration of the final part of the song. It may repeat the final lyrics or build on them in some way. The tag may end loud or soft, depending on the mood that the singers want to create for their audience. Tags not only function as the end or coda of barbershop songs, but they have a life of their own as independent singing vehicles. As mentioned earlier, barbershoppers love to get together and sing tags with their friends and with strangers. It is not uncommon for one singer to know all four parts of a tag (or many tags!) and teach the parts to the people gathered to sing. Tags are also used as vehicles for improving vocal production or for teaching the barbershop style. Tags are invaluable in the barbershop world!
- *Intro*—We have also previously mentioned the introduction, which an arranger may choose to compose to set up the message of the song itself. Intros will usually borrow either textual or musical elements, or both, from the song itself to establish the intro as part of the song. The intro is generally four or eight measures long.
- *Swipe*—The swipe is one of the most important barbershop embellishments. It allows singers to create rhythmic movement within the longer notes. Often instead of just holding a dotted half note for three beats, the singers will create new chords on the second and third beats to keep the harmony interesting and the rhythm moving forward. In a swipe, all the parts generally sing the same

THE BARBERSHOP STYLE

words at the same time. Particularly powerful is the contrary motion swipe, which has some parts moving up while others move downward.

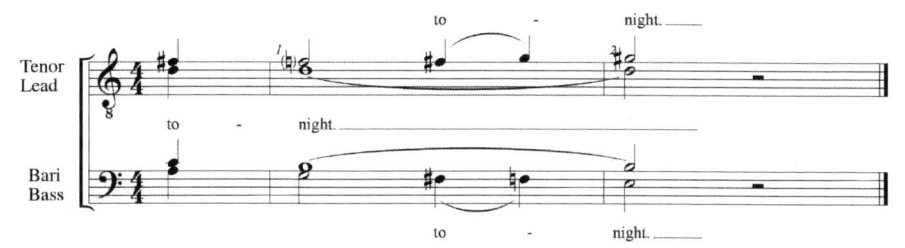

Figure 4.5. Embellishment: Swipe. *Courtesy of the author*

> *Echo*—Sometimes one part will sing a melodic fragment, and this will be echoed by the other parts, using the same or perhaps elaborated words. (See figure 4.5.)
>
> *Bell Chord*—Barbershoppers love bell chords, which are created when chords are broken up so that each part enters one after the other, like bells ringing, until the entire chord is sounding. ♪

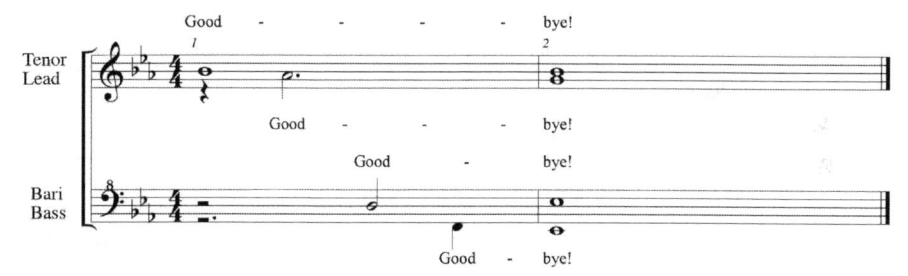

Figure 4.6. Embellishment: Bell chord. *Courtesy of the author*

> *Bari Cherry*—Occasionally on what should be the very last chord of a song, one of the four parts, usually the baritone, will sing the sixth scale step loud and strong before ultimately resolving it to the fifth scale step and allowing the final tonic chord to have its full, ringing sound.
>
> *Unison*—Occasionally, all four parts will sing the same note, either in an exact unison or an octave apart. This can be very effective, since it is an unusual sound in the fabric of four-part chordal harmony.

Peel Off—All parts may begin a phrase in unison and then some parts gradually peel off to different notes, resulting eventually in four-part chords.

Melody Hand-Off—Occasionally, the melody is given temporarily to a part other than the lead to add interest and variety to the song or when a portion of the melody can be more easily handled by the bass or tenor singer.

Solo Passages—Though four-part harmony is the norm in the barbershop style, sometimes variety is achieved by using short solo passages in which one part sings the melody and the other parts sing accompaniment, perhaps on vowel sounds without words. On occasion, a quartet or chorus may wish to feature a member who has an outstanding solo voice. Perhaps a chorus will feature a lead soloist backed up by the chorus in one part of a song. This can be a way for a chorus to feature its director, who may be an outstanding singer but rarely gets to be heard. Quartets love to select an arrangement that features their bass, tenor, or baritone, since normally the lead gets the spotlight. Songs with solos are typically sung for shows or entertainment packages (sets), since in competition the emphasis is on four-part harmony in the traditional barbershop style (lead voice singing melody with three harmony parts).

Patter Background—Sometimes one part is featured singing the melody while the harmony parts sing different words in a rhythmic patter background.

Turn-Around—A turn-around is two or more chords in a progression that lead to a new section or a repeated section.

Key Change—A common device used in barbershop songs is a key change, usually moving the music a half step or a whole step higher to give the song a musical and emotional lift. Normally, the key change occurs after the chorus of the song has been sung through completely. After the key change, the chorus may be partially repeated or embellished, and the song ends with the tag.

Post—Often occurring at the end of the song, a post is a long note that is held by one part while the other three parts sing complex harmonies around the posted note.

THE BARBERSHOP STYLE 63

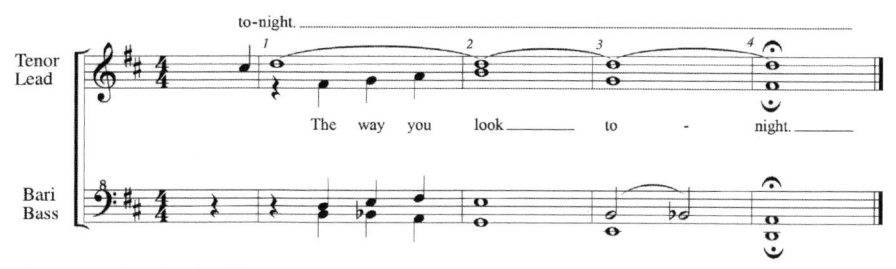

Figure 4.7. Embellishment: Post. *Courtesy of the author*

To reiterate, the main goals of barbershop singing are to lock and ring chords in satisfying harmony and to share a heartfelt message with the listener. "Lock and ring" is best achieved by giving careful attention to four components: accurate tuning, sensitive chord balancing, careful vowel matching, and precise synchronization of words and pitches.

The joy of ringing or, as we say, "busting" chords is somewhat whimsically summed up by the lyrics of one of our favorite songs, sung by both men and women:

The Chordbuster's March[10]

W. A. Wyatt

INTRO
Let's sing a song, let's ring a song, let harmony be true.
Come join the crowd, sing long and loud like chordbusters do.

CHORUS
Let's bust a chord, a good old major chord
With some good close harmony;
Come on and join the fun, we'll bust a minor one,
As we warble merrily.
Let's sing it through again, and then we'll all chime in;
It'll make your heart feel light.
You'll be hoarse tomorrow, but forget your sorrow
While we bust a chord tonight.
If you're a low-down bass, come on and find a place,
And a tenor will be welcome, never fear;
If you sing baritone, no need to stand around alone,

And a lead is what we need right over here.
Let's bust a chord or two, and then you'll know it's true
That a song makes things go right.
Put away your trouble, let your joy be double,
While we bust a chord tonight.

TAG
While we bust a chord tonight!

NOTES

1. Barbershop Harmony Society (BHS), *Barbershop Arranging Manual* (Kenosha, WI: Society for the Preservation and Encouragement of Barbershop Quartet Singing in America, 1980), 3.

2. In music of the Common Practice Period (ca. 1600–1900), the use of chords in parallel motion was discouraged, because it was thought this caused the individual parts to lose their independence. In particular, the use of parallel octaves and fifths was considered displeasing to the ear.

3. Kevin Keller, personal communication, November 22, 2015.

4. For further reading on the subject of tuning, the reader is directed to Ross W. Duffin's book, *How Equal Temperament Ruined Harmony (and Why You Should Care)* (New York and London: Norton, 2008).

5. BHS, *Barbershop Arranging Manual*, 3.

6. Kevin Keller, personal communication, November 22, 2015.

7. Kevin Keller, personal communication, November 22, 2015.

8. Nancy Bergman, "Hurdling the Hazards of the Beginning Arranger" (Sweet Adelines International Education Symposium, San Antonio, TX, 2008), 1.

9. Dale Syverson, "Barbershop Embellishments and Nuances" (Sweet Adelines International Education Symposium, San Antonio, TX, 2008), 1.

10. W. A. Wyatt, *The Chordbuster's March* (words and music). Copyright © 1962 (renewed) by SPEBSQSA, Inc. International copyright secured. All rights reserved. Used by permission.

BIBLIOGRAPHY

Barbershop Harmony Society. *Barbershop Arranging Manual*. Kenosha, WI: Society for the Preservation and Encouragement of Barbershop Quartet Singing in America, 1980.

Bergman, Nancy. "Hurdling the Hazards of the Beginning Arranger." Sweet Adelines International Education Symposium, San Antonio, TX, 2008.

Sweet Adelines International. *Arranger's Guide*. Tulsa, OK: Sweet Adelines International, 1991.

Syverson, Dale. "Barbershop Embellishments and Nuances." Sweet Adelines International Education Symposium, San Antonio, TX, 2008.

5

BARBERSHOP SINGING TECHNIQUE

From Shower to Spotlight

As the barbershop art form has developed over the years and extensive education in the craft has taken place, more and more attention is now given to the vocal technique needed to sing barbershop at a high skill level. This brief chapter can give only a simple overview of some of the vocal practices involved in good barbershop singing. The serious singer will want to broaden his or her knowledge by attending education opportunities devoted to learning to sing well, reading detailed books such as *The Vocal Athlete* by Wendy LeBorgne and Marci Rosenberg or *What Every Musician Needs to Know about the Body* by Barbara Conable and Benjamin Conable, or enrolling in private voice lessons. For now, let us take a look at what a barbershop singer needs to know about vocal technique.

THE AUDITION

Unlike some community or church choirs, barbershop choruses are often auditioned ensembles. This is true because a singer needs certain basic skills in order to be successful as a barbershop singer. When a visitor appears at the door of a barbershop chorus rehearsal, he may be greeted by the membership chairperson and immediately introduced to the director or assistant director, who takes the visitor into a private room for a quick, low-pressure audition. The director will inquire about the singer's music background, which may range from extensive training and experience to singing only in the shower. The guest may be asked to sing a simple, well-known song like "Happy Birthday," perhaps at first singing along with the director but eventually alone. This determines how well the singer can stay in key when singing a cappella. Then the singer may be asked to sing the song in different keys—in the middle, a little lower, a little higher—to determine the tessitura of his voice (the pitch range in which he is comfortable) and singable range. If the singer's voice possesses a rich, low timbre, he is usually encouraged to try out the bass part. If the singer is good at singing in falsetto/head register, he may be encouraged to try out the tenor part. If the singer has a medium-ranged voice and a lot of musical experience, such as playing an instrument or singing in choirs, he may be encouraged to try out the baritone part. And if the singer has a medium-ranged voice and is a confident performer, who seems to enjoy entertaining people, he may be encouraged to try out the lead part, since the leads tell the story of the song. If the person is an inexperienced singer, he also may be encouraged to start on the lead part, since the leads sing the song's melody, which is often easier for less-experienced singers to manage than a harmony part. The visitor is assured that he is not stuck forever on the first part he tries, but that he will be assisted over time to find the most suitable part for his voice. Then the director takes the singer into the main rehearsal room and introduces the singer to the section leader or a strong singer in the part that he will be singing that evening. The section leader or "riser buddy" will then take the singer under his wing and explain the music and other particulars as the rehearsal moves along.

If, during the preliminary audition, it is obvious that a singer cannot match pitches or stay in key at all, the director will gently explain that he is lacking in these skills and would be unable to be successful in singing with this chorus. The director will encourage the singer to seek out a voice teacher and learn to auditate (think the correct pitches in his head in order to be able to sing them accurately), and then the singer is welcome to return to the chorus to audition again. The director may even provide the name of a local singing teacher to assist the person in his quest. The singer may stay for the rehearsal and try singing with the group, but it will quickly become evident to the singer that he lacks the needed skills.

After the successful visitor has sung with the chorus for four to six weeks, found the best part for his voice, and learned a couple of songs, the visitor may indicate that he is ready to audition for membership in the chorus. Typically, the requirements for a membership audition call for the singer to be able to sing a chorus repertory song from memory a cappella, singing all notes and words correctly, and to stay on his part with at least one other person singing it. Some of the more performance-oriented choruses may require that the singer demonstrate the ability to do simple choreography. Auditions can be conducted in several ways. Sometimes a quartet of section leaders sings the song, with the auditioning candidate singing his part along with the quartet. Sometimes the candidate records himself as he sings the song standing in the midst of the chorus and gives the recording to the section leader or director to be critiqued. If the singer fails his audition, he usually tries again in a couple of weeks. When he passes, he is warmly welcomed into the group, and his vocal education begins.

It is certainly true that all choruses do not have the same audition requirements. A small chorus that desperately needs singers may welcome new members without any audition at all, whereas an award-winning chorus, small or large, may have very strict audition requirements. However, there is a place in the barbershop world for many levels of vocal skill, so a singer can and should be persistent about finding a chorus home.

For all intents and purposes, the chorus director is a voice teacher for the members of the chorus. Many directors study voice privately, because they know they need to learn all they possibly can about how the singing voice works. The first part of each rehearsal is usually devoted to vocal warm-up exercises or, as some prefer to call them, vocal skills exercises. Some directors consider this training period so important that they will not allow anyone else to lead it. Others feel that their assistant directors and section leaders should develop experience in leading vocal skills exercises, because this work is so vital to the performance level of the chorus. A twenty-minute period of vocal skills exercises serves as a twenty-minute group voice lesson for each singer in the chorus. Of course, the singers are encouraged to practice and work on both their music and their singing skills at home, and, amazingly, most of them do!

One of the hallmarks of barbershop singers is that they always want to sing better.

ALIGNMENT AND POSTURE

From the beginning, barbershop singers learn that the body is their instrument and that keeping their instrument in the best alignment obtains the best vocal sound. In their book *The Vocal Athlete*, LeBorgne and Rosenberg illustrate that the human skeleton is aligned on a vertical axis and that along that axis there are six major points of balance. Starting from the bottom, the points are (1) ankle joints, (2) knee joints, (3) hip joints, (4) thorax/lumbar spine, (5) arm structure, (6) atlanto-occipital joint (the point where the head perches on top of the spine).[1] When the alignment of these six points is correct, the skeleton is able to support its own weight without the aid of muscles pulling and straining to keep the singer upright. If one moves the body out of alignment, as one must do in the living of life, then the goal should be to re-center one's weight and return to alignment as soon as possible. When proper alignment is maintained, the singing mechanism is free to work efficiently, and a better result is achieved. Also, the body does not tire as easily because there is much less muscle effort present.

Of course, the singer cannot always maintain the ideal alignment when she engages in barbershop choreography moves, but if she is mindful of what constitutes good alignment, she can execute the move so as to hold on to as much of the good posture as possible, and she can return to it immediately following the move. It could be said that the ideal alignment functions like a default position, and the singer will train herself to return there as often as she can.

Exercises

1. Stand in front of a mirror and view your body from the front and from the side. Does it appear to be lined up along a central axis? If not, which of the six points appear to be out of line?
2. Concentrating on the ankle joints, shift your body weight forward onto the balls of your feet, noticing which muscles have to come

into play to keep you standing upright. Then re-center your weight. Shift your weight to your heels, again noticing which muscles are called into play. Return to center. Attempt to stand perfectly centered with your weight completely supported by your ankle joints.
3. Repeat #2 with each succeeding point of balance: knees, pelvic joints, lumbar vertebrae, shoulders, and head. Position each joint further front or back than is desirable, and note the muscular imbalance that occurs. Then come to the point of balance and notice how much more comfortable you are when you are properly aligned.
4. Stand in ideal alignment and note that you feel centered and ready to move in any direction. Then engage in various movements—bending over, sitting, crouching, reaching up, and so on—and attempt to return to centered weight and ideal alignment after each movement.
5. During the week, pay attention to the way you live in your body. Notice if you have a primary challenge—that is, is there one of the six points that is most often out of alignment? Do you have a secondary challenge? Whenever you are able to think about it during each day, return your body to ideal alignment. This position may be new and/or slightly uncomfortable at first if you are not used to it, but over time good alignment will become the most comfortable place to live.

BREATH MANAGEMENT

The desired breathing for singing is the same as for many other athletic endeavors. As described in chapter 2, for inhalation the lower abdomen and ribs expand, allowing the diaphragm to descend, making room for the lungs to fill completely with air. For exhalation, the lower abdomen contracts, allowing the diaphragm to rise and the lungs to empty out the air. In order to create the vocal sound, however, the abdominal muscles must help the vocal folds work to resist the fast exhalation, and therein lies the challenge. Many less-experienced singers complain that they cannot get enough breath for singing. Yet it is often revealed that they are getting plenty of breath when they inhale, but they allow it to escape too fast because they lack the ability to control their exhalation and create efficient phonation. It can help for the singer to work on breathing exercises, such as hissing and singing long notes. But often the singer best learns to control the breath flow by working to produce a strong, clear vocal tone. When the balanced sound is sung, the breath is working properly. Repetition of the beautiful, balanced sounds can build strength, stamina, and good vocal habits.

Exercises

1. Lie on the floor and place a book on your lower abdomen. Inhale, allowing the book to rise (be pushed upward by the expansion of your lower abdomen) in the process. Exhale, allowing the book to fall as the lower abdomen relaxes and the body empties its air. Allow the upper chest muscles to remain relaxed. After a few deep breaths, stand up and place your hand on your lower abdomen in the place that the book previously occupied. Close your eyes and imagine that you are still lying down. Inhale and exhale, allowing your lower abdomen to move out and in as it did when you were lying down.
2. In a standing position, hiss on one breath as follows: *Sh-sh-sh-sh-ssssshhhhh*. Keep your hand on your lower abdomen and allow yourself to feel the movement out and in. Repeat the exercise multiple times. Allow the upper chest muscles to stay relaxed. When you inhale, allow the ribcage and lower body to expand.
3. Sing an [a] vowel on one long pitch, counting mentally as you hold the note and making sure to keep the tone strong and steady. Gradually extend your ability to sustain the tone longer, counting to higher numbers. Experiment with singing different vowels.

BALANCED PHONATION AND RESONATION

As discussed more completely in chapter 2, every musical instrument has (1) a *motor* or energy source, (2) a *vibrator* or sound source, and (3) a *resonator* or sound amplifier. The voice is a wind instrument, so its motor is the breath stream. The basic sound is created when air passes through the vocal folds, tiny membranes located in the larynx. The sound is amplified and takes on a unique timbre when it reaches the spaces of resonation in the vocal tract. A singer striving to improve her singing spends much time attempting to gain direct control of the breath flow and achieve an ideal balance between the pressure of that air as it flows through the folds and the resistance of the folds as they seek to restrain the airflow, thereby creating the beautiful, free vocal sound. Singing teachers refer to this sound as "balanced phonation." A breathy tone indicates too much breath pressure and not enough vocal fold resistance; a tight or pressed tone indicates too much resistance and not enough breath pressure. The beautiful singing voice possesses the ideal balance between breath pressure and resistance, and this is true of the onset, the sustaining, and the release of the tone. In addition, the beautiful sound finds its way unimpeded by constriction into the spaces in the vocal tract that serve as resonators for the voice. This free sound possesses resonance and ring, as it engages the natural overtones that make up sound.

In the article "Resonating with Instant Classic," this international champion men's quartet shared that in their climb to success, resonance matching proved to be their "secret sauce."[2] They explained how they each learned to modify slightly the way they sang certain acoustically related vowels so that the resonance of their four individual voices would achieve a better match and therefore greater lock and ring. Their plan worked well, and they have the medals to prove it.

Exercises

1. Sing a single pitch on a bubble or lip trill. Maintain steady airflow and relaxed lips for as long as each breath lasts. Move this exercise up and down in your range. Sing a five-note scale on the bubble sound, moving up and down in your range. Do the same exercise using the trilled *r*.
2. Sing various vocalises (five-note scales, triads, arpeggios, etc.) through an ordinary drinking straw. Be sure your lips are closed gently around the straw so that no air escapes. Sing your song through the straw. Then remove the straw and sing the song again, maintaining the same strong, steady airflow.
3. Sing the vowels [i], [e], [a], [o], [u] on a single pitch, making sure to maintain an equal resonance space in your throat for all five vowels.

Move this exercise up and down in your range. Chant phrases from your songs on a single pitch, making sure to maintain equal resonance space for each syllable sung. Then sing the melody of your song, maintaining equal resonance space for every syllable.

RANGE AND REGISTERS

A human voice can produce a large range of pitches, from low to high. The entire spectrum of pitches available to a voice is known as the range of the voice. Some voices are naturally more comfortable in a higher pitch range, others in a lower range, and still others prefer a medium pitch range. A trained singing voice may encompass a relatively wide range of pitches, but there is still a portion of the range that feels easier or more comfortable and sounds especially beautiful. This area of the voice is known as the *tessitura* (an Italian word meaning *texture*). The wise barbershop singer most often chooses to sing the part in which his or her voice is naturally the most comfortable.

One of the main tasks for the singer in learning to access a wide range of pitches is to understand the phenomenon of vocal registers. As explained in chapter 2, the voice has two primary modes of vocal fold vibration, which we commonly call registers—mode 1 or chest register and mode 2 or falsetto/head register. Just as a person needs to have two equally strong legs in order to walk smoothly, a singer needs to have two equally strong registers in order to sing efficiently. Thus, much of vocal training centers on helping the singer to become familiar with his or her two registers and learn to "strengthen," "balance," and "mix" them—to mention three terms that one frequently hears during discussion of registration—so that the singer can move easily throughout a wide pitch range and also produce the most appropriate vocal sound to meet the demands of whatever kind of music he or she is singing.

When a singer produces a chest register sound, this calls forth a response in the thyroarytenoid (TA) muscle of the vocal folds. The TA muscle causes the folds to contract into a shorter, thicker configuration. The sound we identify as head register or falsetto occurs when the cricothyroid muscle acts on the larynx, causing the folds to thin and stretch.

BARBERSHOP SINGING TECHNIQUE

A third vocal quality is inherent in the combination of the two registers, and we call this quality "mix." Depending on which muscle is primarily controlling the sound, we may speak of "head mix" (CT-dominant action) and "chest mix" (TA-dominant action).[3] Unless a singer is in the extremes of his or her range, most vocal sounds involve some sort of balancing of the two primary registers.

Jeannette LoVetri, founder of Somatic Voicework—the LoVetri Method, teaches that register balance is the key to good singing. She advocates isolating each register and doing exercises to strengthen it. She states, "Learning to sing in a specific register quality is a very basic vocal skill. Without it certain capacities and abilities will be limited in a singer *forever!*"[4] LoVetri also believes that many vocal problems can be traced to issues related to register balance. "When there are pitch problems, breath problems, volume problems, vowel sound problems, before you look anywhere, LOOK AT REGISTER BALANCE!"[5]

Exercises

1. Exercise your head register by making high, light sounds, such as chicken peeps, puppy whines, or kitten meows. Sing an [i] or [u] vowel on a descending five-note scale, making sure to keep the light, head-register-dominant sound all the way through. Take this sound as low as you can in your range. Try not to engage the chest register.
2. Exercise your chest register by saying "Ho, ho, ho!" in a very low, deep voice. Using a chest-register-dominant quality, sing an ascending three-note scale on the humming consonant [n] at a medium-soft volume. Keep the chest-dominant sound as you go up in your range.
3. Exercise your mix by speaking sentences (or phrases from your songs) in various ranges: low, medium, and high. Pay attention to whether the sounds are chest or head dominant. Then sing the phrases in each range on random pitches, just as if you were speaking them. Explore the different tone qualities available to you as you change the register balance of your mix. Apply these concepts when singing your music.

THE VOCAL DEMANDS OF THE FOUR PARTS

The male lead singer sings in a medium to medium-high range and therefore uses a chest-register-dominant sound that mixes in more head register as he ascends in range. If he has to sing softer high notes, he may use an extremely head-register-dominant mix or even a falsetto sound. The female lead singer sings in a medium range and uses the mix, adjusting the ratio of head register and chest register dominance to the demands of the music. For example, she may use a very head-register-dominant sound in ballad singing but a more chest-register-dominant balance in a loud, peppy uptune. Champion quartet leads often finish an uptune with an exciting, straight-out belt sound that is chest-dominant singing in a very high range.

The baritone singer, both male and female, uses the voice in much the same way as the lead singer, but he or she must pay careful attention to the places in the music where the baritone pitches are higher than the lead pitches. A baritone must sing in such a way as to complement, rather than obscure, the melody line.

Male and female bass singers generally possess a rich, resonant, deep timbre, and they sing primarily in a low range with a very chest-dominant registration. Their high notes are more beautiful and comfortable when they add more head register to the balance as they ascend in range.

The male barbershop tenor may be a true tenor, with easy access to his high notes and a well-balanced head/chest registration. Often, however, a bass or baritone will sing the tenor part because the person has easy access to his falsetto or pure head register. This sound can work well in barbershop, but the pure falsetto sound cannot deliver the power that a blend of chest and head registers can achieve. The female tenor usually possesses a light soprano timbre that can ride above the lead melody without overpowering it. This singer sings in a high range and uses a very head-register-dominant phonation, except when the tenor part occasionally drops below the lead (always indicated in the music with an X above the two notes). In these cases, the tenor must add a little more chest register to her mix to balance the sound properly.

Exercise

1. Visit this book's online resources or the sites of the barbershop organizations and listen to recordings of male and female quartets and choruses. See if you can hear and identify each specific part.

THE VOCAL CHALLENGE OF BARBERSHOP SINGING

Sometimes singers come into the barbershop world having had experience singing other styles of music. Many have sung in school or church choirs or have had solo experience in classical or pop venues. Some have had years of voice lessons and sing very well in certain styles or genres of music. This does not automatically make them good barbershop singers. In fact, they often have to shift gears quite significantly and change some of their vocal habits in order to become good barbershop singers.

Because barbershop music is basically a contemporary commercial music (CCM) style, the barbershop singer primarily needs to employ the vocal techniques of the popular singer rather than the classical singer. Our organizations offer help with this through classes such as championship quartet lead Kim Vaughn's *How to Use Your Classical Training with Barbershop Harmony*, offered at the 2009 Sweet Adelines International Education Symposium. Popular/CCM music uses a speech-like approach with less formal consonants and vowels that are a little less rounded and spacious than in classical singing. The classical singer most often encourages the voice's natural vibrato to be steadily present in every tone. The pop singer uses vibrato as a stylistic device, and the barbershop singer purposely uses very little vibrato in order to help achieve the "lock and ring" sound.

Sometimes a chorus director will have her chorus experiment with singing a phrase or a section of a song in different musical styles—classical, country, jazz, folk—so they can compare genres and get an idea of what sounds are most appropriate to use in barbershop singing.

Singers who have extensive experience in other genres of music and who are uncomfortable with change may decide that barbershop is not for them, and this is perfectly fine. Those who are excited by the challenge of learning to do something new ultimately become the best barbershop singers.

DRAMATIC SKILLS

Last but not least, since vocal music makes use of lyrics as well as musical pitches, the singer is delivering a dramatic message and therefore must possess dramatic or interpretive skills as well as musical and vocal skills. It is not enough simply to make beautiful sounds with the voice. The singer must also have a face that shows emotions, and she must use physical gestures that assist in the telling of the story. Sometimes barbershop singers use "company moves"—that is, planned chorography moves executed by the entire chorus or quartet—that help to convey aspects of the message or story. Most often, however, the singers use "personal moves" or individual gestures that are a natural part of their communicating the story. Performers must learn to use their hands and bodies in a skillful, purposeful, confident manner. In some of the highly skilled, award-winning choruses, the front row may perform complex, even strenuous dance-type chorography while the main body of the chorus does simpler moves in support behind them. The trend in barbershop performance today is to develop choreography that is based in natural-looking gestures that an actor might use to express emotion or emphasize a point. This supports barbershop's primary goal, which is to communicate the message of the lyrics.

Exercises

1. Exercise your face muscles by moving them in an extreme manner. Move all your muscles in all possible directions. Look in the mirror to be sure everything is moving.
2. Isolate different parts of your face and try to move only the muscles in those parts—the top half, the bottom half, the right half, the left half. Observe this activity in the mirror.
3. Flex your face while counting aloud or making random vocal noises. Then flex your face while speaking the text of your song. Finally, flex your face while singing your song. Last but not least, sing your song and allow your face to have strong facial expressions that communicate the meaning of the text.
4. Recite the text of your song as a dramatic monologue, using appropriate facial expressions and gestures. Then sing your song using appropriate facial expressions and gestures.

THE CONSUMMATE BARBERSHOP SINGER

Barbershop singing is for all ages and all levels of singers. At the minimum, it requires the musical ability to sing an independent vocal part a cappella in combination with three other parts. To sing barbershop well, the singer needs to develop enough vocal skill to sing his or her part with a pleasing sound and relative ease. The goal of singing barbershop at a very high skill level can offer singers as much challenge as singing in any other vocal music genre. ♪

In her Sweet Adelines regional training course titled *A Crash Course in Vocal Production*, coauthor Diane Clark enumerates eight characteristics of a good singer:

> (1) appropriate body alignment and physical balance; (2) adequate breath management—both acquisition and utilization; (3) efficient, balanced phonation—clear, focused tone quality; (4) strong development of individual head and chest registers and the ability to mix the two in various adjustments; (5) full resonance that is consistent in all vowels; (6) clarity of diction in whatever language is being sung (e.g., Standard American English) with independence of jaw and tongue; (7) balanced and effective use of expressive tools: face, voice, gesture and body language; (8) stamina to maintain a consistent high level of efficient, effective performance.[6]

Obviously, to become proficient in all these areas takes a lifetime of study and practice.

Our barbershop organizations are now well populated with trained professional and amateur musicians who have achieved success in many styles of singing. This has served to bring education and quality to the barbershop world and raised the standards for the art form. As the current saying goes, "It's not your grandfather's barbershop." Singers at all levels find that today's barbershop singing challenges them to sing their very best, and they are eager to rise to the task.

NOTES

1. Wendy LeBorgne and Marci Rosenberg, *The Vocal Athlete* (San Diego, CA: Plural, 2014), 4.

2. Scott Kitzmiller, "Resonating with Instant Classic," *Harmonizer*, May/June 2016, 18–19.

3. Jeannette LoVetri, *Somatic Voicework—the LoVetri Method, Level I Workshop Manual* (Albion, MI: Albion College, 2009), 17.

4. LoVetri, *Somatic Voicework*, 18.

5. LoVetri, *Somatic Voicework*, 18.

6. Diane M. Clark, *A Crash Course in Vocal Production* (N.p.: Sweet Adelines International Region 2 Area School, 2010), 1.

BIBLIOGRAPHY

Clark, Diane M. *A Crash Course in Vocal Production*. N.p.: Sweet Adelines International Region 2 Area School, 2010.

Conable, Barbara, and Benjamin Conable. *What Every Musician Needs to Know about the Body*. Portland, OR: Andover Press, 1998.

Kitzmiller, Scott. "Resonating with Instant Classic." *Harmonizer*, May/June 2016.

LeBorgne, Wendy D., and Marci D. Rosenberg. *The Vocal Athlete*. San Diego, CA: Plural, 2014.

LoVetri, Jeannette. *Somatic Voicework—the LoVetri Method, Level I Workshop Manual*. Albion, MI: Albion College, 2009.

6

BARBERSHOP ENSEMBLES

You Can't Do It Alone

The basic unit of the barbershop style is, of course, the quartet. In fact, the official name of the seminal barbershop organization remains the Society for the Preservation and Encouragement of Barbershop Quartet Singing in America, better known today as the Barbershop Harmony Society. Although there is much satisfaction to be found in duets, trios, and ensembles with five or more separate vocal lines, it's the quartet that this style finds most satisfying. As described elsewhere in this book, while triads function quite well with their three separate tones (root/R, third, fifth), it's from the major-minor seventh and, to a lesser extent, the major-minor ninth chord that barbershop gets its distinctive characteristic sound. The four pitches of this chord (R, 3, 5, flat 7) generate a harmonic tension (most often producing a resolution to a chord, the root of which is a fifth below) and a resonance, which, when properly tuned, balanced, and sung with matching vowel sounds, produce the "lock and ring" that barbershoppers live for.

That said, it is true today, and probably has been true for most of the history of organized barbershop singing, that most singers find their harmony not in a quartet but in a larger ensemble called a *chorus*. (In the barbershop world, the term *choir* is not used.) Every barbershop chapter around the world—and chapters number in the thousands now—meets regularly and sings together as a chorus. Small, large, in-between—our hobby is a choral one. The four-part nature of the style remains in place; there are just several folks singing your part with you, much as in traditional SATB (Soprano, Alto, Tenor, Bass), SSAA (Soprano 1, Soprano 2, Alto 1, Alto 2), or TTBB (Tenor 1, Tenor 2, Baritone, Bass) ensembles.

So you want to sing barbershop. How, then, do you find other singers with whom to do it? The first and most obvious answer is to attend a meeting of a chapter of one of the existing organizations in your area. With over sixteen hundred local chapters, male and female, in North America and hundreds of others scattered around the globe, an Internet search (see appendix B) should quickly produce the location and details of meetings of a barbershop chapter near you. While individual results may vary, in the great majority of chapters you will be welcomed as a valued guest, given a book of music, assigned a "riser buddy," shown where you should sit or stand, and generally be asked to join in the fun! After a time, if you want to try your hand in a quartet, you will be able to find like-minded singers there who will help you form a group.

If no chapter exists in your area or if you fail to find suitable quartet mates at the chapters you visit, take heart. It's quite likely that there are other singers who are not yet singing this addictive style out there searching for you! The usual Internet routes—Craig's List, search engines, and so on—as well as analogue methods such as newspaper notices, tearaway sheets at local music stores, supermarkets, churches, and so on, may prove to be successful. A perusal of area church choirs, amateur theaters, civic chorus rolls, and the like, may be effective, too. The most important thing is to be persistent. You will doubtless find other singers who are not right for your new ensemble, but if you persist you can and will be able to create a quartet.

However, finding three other singers is not the most difficult part of the process. Finding three others whose natural voices match well, who have the ranges necessary for all four parts, who share your desire to improve individually and as an ensemble, and with whom you enjoy spending lots—*lots*—of time may challenge even the most dedicated and persistent searcher. But please persist. Success in this area—creating a barbershop quartet of some reasonable skill level—will give you and all the members of the quartet countless hours of enjoyment.

Figure 6.1. Voices Incorporated Chorus. Courtesy of the Pacific Northwest WA Chapter, Barbershop Harmony Society

Elsewhere the parts are described more fully, but we think it's important to list the basic personality and vocal types that work best for each part here as well.

Lead: The lead singer needs to be just that—a vocal, musical, and charismatic leader. He or she will be the voice most heard, the face most viewed, and the body language most observed. It has been said that the lead part—the melody of the song—is the easiest part to learn and the hardest part to sing. And it is difficult to sing correctly. The lead singer must possess a clarity of tone, a uniformity of vocal quality, an understanding of the story or theme of the song, and an ability to "sell" the song throughout his or her range. A good lead singer is not easily found—and inevitably compromises must be made—but this is the most important voice in the quartet. Choose it well.

Bass: The bass singer must first have the range to sing the part effortlessly. Low or high, the voice must provide the resonance necessary for the barbershop sound, the smoothness of line that allows the ensemble to ride on his or her "river of sound," and the musicianship to balance his or her part of the chord properly. The second most obvious part to the listener, this singer must also have the showmanship necessary to communicate the emotion and story of the song to the audience.

Baritone: This is the part that probably requires the best "ear" in the quartet. The successful baritone will sing almost effortlessly, balance his or her part with greater volume on roots and fifths and less on thirds and sevenths, use more volume below the melody and less above, tune to the overtone series, and match vowel sounds so as to fill the chord without being really heard by the audience. A skilled and talented baritone goes almost unnoticed, while a poor one is always heard—a distraction at best, an ensemble killer at worst. And while he or she is making all of these important adjustments for the good of the ensemble, the baritone must also engage the audience visually. The audience may not hear the baritone, but they will certainly see him or her.

Tenor: Another "tuning" part, the tenor sings mostly thirds and flat sevenths, so he or she must know and feel the relative tuning required by each. Always light—men often use falsetto here—the tenor part must "fit" the ensemble much in the way the baritone does. The tenor voice is always present but almost never noticeable (except when appropriate for interest or when singing the occasional short melody part). And, of course, the visual aspect of the performance must be accomplished, too. The audience sees the whole ensemble. Everyone must be a showman to make the performance successful.

Sound like an impossible task? To find four people who possess the appropriate ranges; who have—or are willing to acquire—the necessary knowledge and skill; who share your hopes, expectations, and aspirations of excellence; and who can be around each other for a good portion of their free time each week is difficult. Fear not! It's difficult but certainly not impossible. Hundreds, perhaps thousands, of successful quartets exist. Yours can be one of them.

OK, you've found three other friends, and you want to create a quartet. What next? First, select a time and place to meet. Successful groups meet regularly—at least once a week—and rehearse in a place that is quiet and in which they will be undisturbed. Pets, children, spouses, or friends who constantly intrude into the rehearsal process will make a challenging task even more difficult. Select a place away from the disturbances of life. Next, what music will you sing? Most new ensembles begin with material that's too difficult for them. Do not make this mistake. Learning your parts and rehearsing the ensemble to achieve proper tuning, voice blending, balance, synchrony, and so on is a difficult thing to get right. If the material is too difficult—too fast, too "rangy," too angular (too many difficult skips in one or more parts)—the task will be more challenging than it needs to be. Carefully look over the arrangements you find. Are the parts easily within the range of each singer? Are the parts free of too many large jumps from note to note? Do all of you like the song? If the answer to these questions is yes, then it may be the song/arrangement for you.

How do you find music? The barbershop organizations listed elsewhere in this book all have music publishing departments that have hundreds of arrangements for sale. And the Internet has scores of websites of arrangers who sell their work. Just be careful to preview any arrangement you think you might like.♪ If it's too hard for your new ensemble, barbershop singing will not be as fun for you as it should be as quickly as it could be. After you've gained experience and skill at singing and performing this rewarding style, you can progress to more challenging material.

While a long compendium of rehearsal techniques is not in the purview of this book—many resources for rehearsal techniques are available from the several barbershop organizations—it might be helpful to list a few basic rehearsal techniques here. First, each singer must be able to sing his or her part with confidence and accuracy. This is a four-part art form, and each part must be sung well. First, know your part cold! Come to rehearsals ready to sing it without reliance on anyone else. Be able to sing it against the other parts without being drawn off your note. Only in this way will quick, satisfying progress in the ensemble be possible. Second, everyone should sing the melody together in unison until the song and the collective interpretation of the song is known to all four singers. Then sing duets between each part in every combination on short phases. While each pair is singing, the other two singers listen and offer constructive, caring, helpful suggestions for improvement. Listen for solidarity, tuning, synchrony, and vowel-sound match as you do this. Then put the ensemble together on the section of the arrangement being rehearsed, and when it sounds good to you, move to the next part of the song. In this carefully planned and executed way, good music and good fun will follow.

To hearken back to the beginning of this chapter, though, you may find that chorus singing is for you. If so, this short list of good habits of the successful chorister may prove helpful:

1. To the extent that you can, learn your music outside of rehearsal. Learning tracks (which have your part predominant against the other three) are often available for this purpose.
2. Be regular in attendance.
3. Always be early to rehearsal. Be in your place ready to sing *before* the director is ready to start.
4. Be in your spot, ready to sing, before the break is over.
5. Come with a pencil and a bottle of water. Mark the director's wishes in your music with the pencil. Hydrate often, as this is vital for vocal health.
6. Don't wear perfume or cologne. Bathe often. You are usually in tight quarters—sometimes in a warm room—for an extended period of time. Be courteous to your fellow choristers.

BARBERSHOP ENSEMBLES

7. Don't talk. Listen. Be prepared to sing when the director wants you to sing. Your witty remarks, while appropriate and appreciated in many places, are distractions at a rehearsal.
8. Mind your own business. Your riser mates will take care of themselves.
9. Smile. This is *fun!*
10. Help clean up, put chairs and risers away, police the area after the rehearsal is finished.

Sometimes it can be frustrating for a singer if he or she can't find three other people with whom to sing barbershop. It is certainly true that you can't do it alone. But this fact is also the source of much camaraderie and fellowship, which is a huge part of the attraction of barbershop singing.

Figure 6.2. Fenton Lakes Chorus. *Courtesy of E. R. Lilley Photography*

❼
SINGING AS ONE VOICE
Techniques for Achieving Unit Sound

In chapter 5, we looked at some concepts and exercises that the individual singer can use to develop the vocal technique needed to sing good barbershop. In this chapter, we will examine some approaches used by directors and coaches to help barbershop ensembles achieve the elusive "unit sound," sometimes described as singing with one voice. Every choral director in any genre hopes for talented and capable ensemble members with good voices and some ability to make beautiful vocal sounds. In the barbershop world, directors expect to work with singers who have these traits plus a good ear for singing harmony. From that point, in the weekly rehearsal directors teach their singers how to improve their individual vocal production and to mold their voices into a unified, blended, synchronized sound. There are hundreds of exercises and tools that may be used; this chapter will focus on a representative sample. ♪

BREATH MANAGEMENT AND FORWARD MOTION

One of the best exercises to help singers learn to breathe using their abdominal muscles is the simple act of blowing up balloons. If the singers blow up their balloons a few times during a warm-up session, they automatically start to exercise the key muscles that control the lungs and the activity of the vocal folds. From there, it is an easy transition to having them inhale and then resist the fast exhalation while they sing. The muscle antagonism that is generated by this exercise helps to strengthen the abdominal muscles and build their stamina.

Another way to develop improved breath management is to have the singers vocalize semi-occluded (partially closed) sounds. They can vocalize on singable consonants such as [m], [n], [v], [z], or [l] or vocalize lip trills and trilled [r] exercises. Because the vocal tract is partially obstructed by the articulation of the consonant, the singers' abdominal muscles have to work a little harder to create and sustain the sound.

Singers in a chorus are sometimes asked to sustain longer phrases than some of the individual singers are able to do. Thus, singers must learn a technique called, variously, "private," "sneak," or "stealth" breathing. That is, each singer must take periodic breaths within the phrase without letting the audience know this is happening. There are a number of things to remember to make this work easily. First, breathe deeply so that the lower abdomen expands, rather than using the more easily visible and less-efficient high chest breath. Second, keep mouthing the words while inhaling, so that the singer appears to be singing all the while. Third, breathe *before* a breath is needed and *not* in the obvious places, such as after long notes. It takes some practice to acquire this skill, so choruses work on it specifically. The director may have the group silently mouth the words to a well-known song such as "Row, Row, Row Your Boat" or "Happy Birthday" while continuously inhaling and exhaling. Next, the chorus can sing the song, having each singer take intermittent breaths (more than usual), while continuing to mouth the words. The goal is to not let anyone see that you have taken a breath midphrase. Sometimes it is helpful to leave out a syllable (and a note) in the middle of a word in order to "catch" a breath. The secret is to make all of this as smooth and unnoticeable, visually and aurally, as possible.

Often less-experienced singers tend to run out of air or fail to sustain the energy at the ends of their phrases, and this creates dead time or white space between phrases, causing the music to bog down. To maintain forward motion in the music, singers work on various ways to keep entire phrases strong and to propel themselves energetically from one phrase to the next. One such tool is to crescendo in every phrase, making the last word or syllable the strongest. Another useful exercise is to make the release of each phrase the inhalation for the next phrase, so that there is immediate movement from one thought to another, just as one moves in a spoken conversation. A third tool is to crescendo slightly on every long note, which helps to keep energy in every phrase and forward motion in the song as a whole. Generally, if the singer feels that each phrase has "shape" (is energized to a high point and, perhaps, relaxed toward the end) and "direction" (moves toward the next phrase and connects, emotionally, with it), the song moves forward, pitch is maintained, phrases are sustained, and a musical product is created.

Since barbershop groups use choreography, it can be helpful to develop a choreography move that physically supports the sustaining of the end of a phrase and moves the singer quickly to the initiation of the next phrase. For example, an arm being lifted reminds the singer to keep the breath energy moving all the way to the end of the phrase.

STANDARD AMERICAN ENGLISH

The model language for barbershop singing is Standard American English, which very few people speak. One of the challenges for every chorus is to overcome the ever-present regional accents, which often include some very poor speech habits, and to bring the ensemble into singing a common language that is tuneful to the ears. First and foremost, directors must convince their singers to sing primarily on vowels, rather than consonants, since vowels carry the essence of the vocal sound. In addition, vowel purity or integrity must be maintained in order to encourage beauty and unity of tone. Therefore, we speak of singing and sustaining target vowels. That is, one vowel sound and shape must be sustained from the beginning to the end of each syllable, and in the case of diphthongs, the secondary vowels must be delayed until the very last moment. Because people tend to sing with less-than-perfect speech habits, singers must be conditioned to sustain and maintain target vowels. It is often true that singers from countries where English is not the first language sing better English than native English speakers who have many poor speech habits to overcome. If all singers can learn to move quickly through their consonants, reach their target vowels quickly, and sustain them for the full length of each syllable, the group will have a more synchronized sound, which is a primary goal in barbershop singing, because this enhances opportunities to "lock and ring." This is also why singers must sing clean, accurate sounds on each pitch so that the notes of each chord are well tuned.

CHORD BALANCING

One of the most important concepts aiding in achieving lock and ring is chord balancing. As pointed out in earlier discussions, reinforcing the natural overtone series is the key to successful barbershop singing, and therefore it is necessary to sing the fundamental pitch louder than other higher pitches to achieve this goal. Typically, the part singing the root of a chord should be the loudest; the fifth should be the next strongest in volume, with the third next, and the sixth, seventh, or ninth at the least volume. Singing this way would be a challenge even for well-trained professional singers. How can amateur singers learn to do it? Fortunately, because barbershop music basically uses eleven chords and barbershop arrangements are written with chord voicing that enhances lock and ring, the singers can become quite familiar with the traditional patterns of barbershop chords and can learn how to balance them properly. The director or section leader can help the singers to mark their music so that, with experience, they can learn to hear and feel when they are on the fundamental note (the root) or a harmony note (all the others). The more highly skilled the chorus or quartet, the more adept they will be at chord balancing. It is a goal toward which all good groups strive.

RESONANCE AND VOWEL MATCHING

Another goal for barbershop ensembles is to achieve matching resonance, and this is often approached through the challenge of vowel matching. Because people's vocal habits are different, not everyone will naturally have the same amount of space for a [u] vowel, and in some parts of the country, this vowel may be thin, pinched, or twangy. Directors seek to help their singers find a consistent resonance space for all their vowels, which leads to a more unified choral sound.

A favorite tool for understanding vowels is the 3-D vowel system. This system is based on the idea that our main resonator, the pharynx or throat, can be pictured as a big room with three dimensions—width, height, and depth. Ideally, we would like to be resonating all our vowels in all three dimensions all the time. We can also understand the vowel spectrum as being composed of three groups:

the wide vowels—[i] [ɪ] [e] [ɛ] [æ]
the tall vowels—[a] [ʌ]
the deep vowels—[ɔ] [o] [ʊ] [u]

When singing a vowel that is naturally wide, like [i], we do not have to worry about the particular dimension that is inherent in the vowel, but we may find that our [i] is not tall enough or deep enough to have full resonance. Thus, we may need to add the dimensions that are missing in order to fill out the sound. We can say that the role-model vowels for the three dimensions are [i] for width, [a] for height, and [o] for depth. If a singer sings a dark and covered [u] vowel, the director may suggest, "Put a little more [i] into your [u]." In other words, add the missing dimension to your sound. With a bit of practice, singers can learn to become more aware of the need to have all the available resonance space open and ready to use while singing any vowel. Some people like to refer to the 3-D vowel system as the cathedral vowel system. If you imagine a spacious Gothic cathedral with marvelous acoustics, you note the transepts (width), the dome and crypt (height), and the nave and chancel (depth). The goal is to resonate your vowels in all parts of the cathedral (pharynx).

Another tool that can help with vowel matching is the "pencil in the teeth," or you can use your pinky finger, which you insert between your upper and lower teeth at the side of your mouth. When you sing, do not allow the teeth to stop touching the pencil or finger; the teeth simply rest gently against the pencil. Because the jaw is not allowed to open, the singer is required to create space for the vowels inside the pharynx, and this helps to achieve a more consistent resonance for every vowel. It also makes diction much clearer and easier to understand because every vowel is clear and authentic.

ACHIEVING BLEND

Some misunderstand the concept of blending to mean that individual voices are manipulated to sound like the other voices in the ensemble. This is not the best approach. The most desirable choral sound occurs when each individual singer is singing at her best, while monitoring the way she fits her voice into the unit. One tool that can be used here is the concept of the role-model vowel. Almost every singer has one vowel that naturally sounds the best—produces the richest, fullest, most resonant, ringing tone—in her voice. Individuals can discover their best or role-model vowel and then work to match their other vowels to it. Some of the most amazingly rich ensemble singing is produced when the director asks each singer to sing a pitch or a phrase on her role-model vowel. This sound gives a hint of the potential of the ensemble to blend all the voices into a vibrant unit.

Other efforts to achieve blend may focus on having the singers create matching resonance in their vowels. The champion quartet Instant Classic describes their success with doing this in chapter 5.

TUNING

Tuning properly is, of course, essential in all musical ensembles, and all chorus directors know that to tune properly, good vocal production, well-matched vowels and resonances, proper chord balancing, and synchronized movement from note to note—from chord to chord—are necessary. Barbershoppers pay particular attention to all of these things to enhance our chances of success with "lock and ring," and to help with this, it's important for barbershoppers to know just what it means to be "in tune."

So what does it mean to be in tune? Listening carefully to two pitches sounded simultaneously will reveal the answer. When a unison—or any consonant interval between two pitches—is perfectly in tune, the "noise" in the sound disappears. The sound becomes "clean" and "clear." When the unison or interval is out of tune, muddiness is apparent; there are "beats" in the sound. There is one beat per second, in fact, for every cycle per second that the two pitches are away from "perfect" intonation.

In chapter 4, the harmonic series and the various scales and methods of tuning employed in Western music are discussed. For our purposes here, we can simply state that there are two general types of tuning used in barbershop, which may be called *horizontal* and *vertical* tuning. Horizontal tuning is used by the melody singers, usually the leads. It closely approximates the "well-tempered" tuning of a keyboard. That is, each half step is almost exactly the same "size." Vertical tuning is used by the harmony singers—the tenors, baritones, and basses. This tuning is generally based on the intervals found in the naturally occurring harmonic series (see chapter 4)—the intervals that sound "clean" when tuned according to the notes contained in the harmonic series of the lower, louder note.

Melody singers, as we have said, mostly use the pitches on the piano. If they didn't, the melody would sound pretty strange to us. We are used to the melodies played on the piano, and this is what we expect to hear when a song is sung. Each pitch is related to the pitch that comes before and after it, hence horizontal tuning. Just to make life more difficult, however, our melody singers do occasionally have to adjust their pitches beyond what is determined by the melody alone to maintain the tonal center—the key of the passage being sung. Due to an acoustical effect known as the Pythagorean comma, if the melody is not retuned upward at key spots, the overall key of the song will sag. (While this is a primary responsibility of the melody singers, all members of the ensemble must help lift the key throughout the performance, too.)

Harmony singers have a somewhat different job. As they sing in harmony to the melody, they must choose pitches from the harmonic series of the root of the chord being sung. This means that each pitch is not related to the pitch that comes before or after it but rather to the melody note being sung—hence the name vertical tuning. And as stated above, harmony singers also must occasionally help to "lift" the key to maintain a consistent tonal center throughout the song. Learning to sing in tune in this way requires both knowledge and skill. Many singers simply haven't realized that their note in fact can be higher or lower than the note of the keyboard that corresponds to the note on the page.

Some Rehearsal Techniques to Improve Tuning

1. Make sure that the vowels are pure, clear, and uniform across the ensemble.
2. Ask the leads to sing against a steady pitch sounded in the key of the phrase. (This often changes throughout the song, even when

the key signature doesn't change. For instance, many B sections of an AABA song are in a different, though related, key from that of the A sections.)
3. Ask the leads to sing without the steady pitch but to refer back to it often or occasionally, depending on the skill level of the singers. This trains them to audiate and repeat the key center as they sing.
4. Sing all the duets between parts, not only the obvious lead/bass duet but other combinations as well. Try tenors and basses together, leads and baritones, and leads and tenors. The tenor/baritone duet is less helpful, since they both frequently sing harmony rather than fundamental notes, but it's fun and challenging. Try it occasionally.
5. Find the octaves that occur between any two parts. Stop the ensemble and make sure that these are in tune. You'll probably find that the upper octave needs to be raised a bit, stretching the octave, to achieve the best intonation and pitch maintenance.
6. Train all the singers to listen while they sing. This may sound intuitive, but experience has shown that many singers listen mostly to themselves, not experiencing and consequently not understanding how their sound and pitch fits in with the singers around them. Critical listening while also attending to healthy vocal technique, free and resonant sound production, accurate vowel formation, precise synchronization, the emotional content of the lyric, and the choreography is not easy. It is a habit that must be developed over a significant period of time.

There are a couple of other things that singers can learn to do to help with the tuning of the ensemble. The fifth of a chord in barbershop tuning is slightly higher in pitch than that of the same note played on a piano. Because of this, if every harmony singer who has the fifth of a chord sings it on the "high" side—that is, gently lifts the pitch a few cycles—the chord will tune better, and the tonal center will more likely be maintained. Obviously, it is not feasible to focus on the fifth of every chord being sung, but starting with identifying this part of the chord in the longer notes will help the ensemble be more successful. Since the fifth of the chord is frequently in the bass part, basses who learn to identify and lift this pitch will have a particularly positive effect on the tuning of the ensemble. Quite often, the bass note is the fifth of a dominant seventh (*re* in the tonic scale). The late Dr. Val Hicks, a longtime barbershopper and noted music educator, often said that our basses don't know where *re* is. Learning to consistently lift this pitch will gradually dispel that notion.

It is helpful for basses, as it is for all singers, to know that while two successive notes may share the same name, they are often two different pitches. For instance, in the barbershop polecat song "Down Our Way," the second and third notes in the first measure (on the words *our way*) are both Ds, but the first is the root of a D7 chord and the second is the fifth of a G7 chord. To keep the tonal center in key, the second of these notes must be sung higher than the first. As this pattern is often found in barbershop literature, it will pay basses to be aware of it.

Dr. Val Hicks often worked with ensembles on tuning the perfect fifth. It was his view that this is the most important interval of all those we sing, and as most of our chords contain this interval somewhere within them, it is helpful to work on tuning this interval properly. Val provided us with twenty exercises to develop our ability to sing this important interval in tune, included in this book as appendix D. We recommend them to you. Persistent practice will produce more accurate intonation and from that, more of the all-important lock and ring of barbershop.

Melody singers can help the tonal center by lifting the pitch of the "leading tones." These are the seventh degree of the scale of the key and, somewhat less obviously, the third scale degree, as well. While it is true that the third in a chord tuned to "just" intonation (the tuning we use that utilizes the harmonic series of the root of the chord being sung) is in fact lower than the same note played on a keyboard, lifting the third of the chord results in a pleasing, bright sound and helps maintain the tonal center, too. In our view, this is because the third of a barbershop-seventh chord is the "leading" tone to the chord to which it leads as we progress through our harmony via the circle of fifths. So ask your singers to slightly raise the pitch of the fifths and thirds of the main chords—the ones with the longer duration—and you'll be pleasantly surprised by the results in the intonation of the group, chorus and quartet alike.

RISER PLACEMENT

It is certainly true that the sound of any ensemble is affected by the way the singers are positioned. This positioning has a huge effect on the way the singers sing. When one stands next to a fully resonant voice, one is usually inspired to sing with a more resonant sound. And certain voices seem to bring out or enhance other voices in their vicinity, while some voices clash when they stand together. Often a coach is asked to help place the singers on the risers to achieve the most desirable sound. This may mean that the coach will listen to every voice in each section and determine which voices sound best where. There are many systems or methods for arranging people on the risers. One method is called the theory of threes. In this method, three singers on the same part stand shoulder to shoulder with the strongest and best voice in the middle so that the other two singers can match the good sound. Then the groups of three can be arranged in a variety of ways on the risers, but the threesome always will be an anchor for each other.

Another successful method categorizes the singers by timbre or vocal quality. In a large chorus, one might use the numbers 1 through 5, but in most small or medium-sized groups, the numbers 1 through 3 are sufficient. By sections, the director hears each voice and assigns each singer a number. The number 3 people have a richer, darker, heavier timbre. The number 1 singers have a lighter, brighter, edgier timbre. The number 2 singers have a solid, mellow, warm timbre. One approach has the number 3 singers stand at the back, the number 2 singers in front of them, and the number 1 singers at the very front of the chorus, allowing the richer, fuller sounds to provide a cushion for the lighter, brighter ones. Another approach has the most resonant singers (the number 3s) stand in the middle of the chorus, with the number 2s split to the outside of them and the number 1 singers on the outside edges. This can be done with each section, if the chorus stands in sections, or over the entire chorus, if the various parts are scattered (or "shotgunned") across the risers. This creates a "power alley" of strong, resonant singers singing more directly at the audience since the risers are curved. Of course, if there is a dancing front row in a chorus, the director must be careful about the voices chosen for the front row. Voices on the front row that are too big or strong may stick out of the group sound, so care must be taken to keep things in balance.

STANDING ORDER FOR QUARTETS

The order in which members of a quartet stand has a noticeable effect on their overall vocal sound. The most common positioning for quartets is to have the lead and the bass stand next to each other on the inside, with the baritone beside the bass and tenor beside the lead. This matches the natural duets within the quartet and allows the main harmony singers (the tenor and baritone) to more easily tune their part to the predominant voices in the quartet. However, certain voices are enhanced by standing next to each other, and certain standing arrangements can cause particular voices to come alive in the fabric of the sound. Often a coach will spend a good bit of time experimenting with a quartet's standing order, until he or she achieves the positioning that makes the group sound their very best.

LEARNING A NEW SONG

In this modern age of technology, most barbershoppers learn their new songs from professionally made learning tracks, which include their individual part and opportunities to sing their part with the other three parts. However, occasionally there is a need for a song to be learned right in the chorus rehearsal. One useful approach is to have the section leaders ready to teach the song, and working the music in small, manageable sections is helpful. The lead section leader sings the lead part, while the other leads listen and audiate. Then all leads join and sing that segment a few times until it is secure. Next the bass section leader sings the bass part, and the other basses listen and audiate. After the basses have sung their part a couple of times, the leads can join in, humming their part. This practice is continued, adding the baritones and the tenors, with each new part being sung and the already-learned parts being hummed. Finally, when everyone knows his or her part, the entire group can sing the words at full volume. Then the group moves on and learns another section of the song the same way.

Once a song has been well learned, it can be made more secure by having chorus members form the sides of a square (or a triangle, in the case of smaller groups), making sure all four parts are represented in each side. The director stands in the center and faces one side, which begins to sing the song. When the director turns at random and faces a different group, they instantly take over the singing, and this continues throughout the song. This is a challenging exercise, which requires the singers to know the song well and to be able to audiate efficiently while the other segments are singing so that they can step in without hesitation.

COMMUNICATING THE STORY: THE MESSAGE OF THE LYRICS

Every song has a message in the lyrics that is, ideally, enhanced by the musical setting. Some would say that the main point of singing a song is to communicate the story or message of the song to the audience. However, it is often true that singers learn a song and never really take a close look at what the lyrics have to say.

A very useful approach to learning a song involves typing out the text as poetry and memorizing the words before ever looking at the musical notes of the song. The singer can recite the lyrics as a dramatic monologue and discover what the story is and what emotions are present in each section. It can be useful to work with the idea of emotion clusters for each section. For example, the introduction of the song "Basin Street Blues" states, "I'm gonna take a trip down on that sailing ship, and I'd like to have ya all join in." A cluster of emotions (usually three) for this opening section might be "anticipating, excited, determined." Right away the singer has an appropriate emotional idea of how to begin the song. The verse then states, "Won't ya come along with me to the Mississippi?" The emotion cluster might be "inviting, hopeful, happy." The sections of the poem usually indicate where a change of emotions is needed. This song has nine sections, so the singer would end up working with nine emotional clusters. The storyteller makes an emotional journey from the beginning of the song to the end, and working with the text in this way helps the singer understand that journey better. After the singer is comfortable with the lyrics and the story, she or he can add the music, which will typically enhance the message already established.

COMMUNICATING EMOTIONS: THE PROJECTIVE MODES

The singer may possess a heartfelt understanding of the story, but the audience cannot read his or her thoughts or look within his or her mind to get that message. The audience can only understand the message through three modes of expression: the sound of the singer's voice, the singer's facial expressions, and the singer's gestures and body language.

The great teacher of singer-actors Dr. H. Wesley Balk referred to these tools as the projective modes—that is, the three means by which the performer projects meaning to the audience.[1] Some performers are more naturally at home using facial expressions; others use their voices more easily; and some are quite kinesthetically inclined, "talking with their hands" and using a great deal of body language. The skilled singer-actor, however, needs to become skilled at using all three projective modes so that a stronger message is communicated to the audience. Thus, exercises are needed to help performers develop these skills.

Chapter 5 suggests some facial-flexing exercises to develop flexibility. Another useful approach is to work with emotional attitudes and learn to express a large variety of attitudes with the face. Making grotesque masks can help the muscles become more comfortable expressing emotions in a bigger way. Have the singers take a huge, exaggerated mask and hold it for fifteen seconds, then release it quickly. Call out one emotion, such as joy, fear, anger, surprise, and so on, and do each emotion in succession—fifteen seconds each. This helps the singers gain a greater ability to show emotions to the very back of a large performance space. After the singers are comfortable using their faces to express emotions, they can recite the spoken lyrics and practice expressing their chosen emotion clusters with their faces as they speak. Ultimately, they can learn to sing the song with the same strong facial expressions.

When a singer has a particular emotion or feeling in mind, the sound of his or her voice changes. Speaking or singing from the idea of "sad" brings a melancholy tone to the vocal sound and helps the audience understand what emotion the speaker is experiencing. Vocal exercises can be done with emotional cues so that singers learn to allow their voices to achieve a greater variety of vocal color and emotional nuance. The chorus can sing a five-note scale exercise, and the director can give a different emotional cue for each pattern. This gets the singers in the habit of singing with feelings, not just making mechanical, robotic sounds.

Finally, the singers must become more comfortable using gestures and body language to help convey their meaning. They can take short segments of the song text and speak them, using different gestures to help make their point. They might say the phrase "Ya know the band's there to meet us" ten times, using a different gesture each time. Or they can say the phrase at a low level of body involvement and increase the body action with each succeeding repetition of the phrase. These exercises will probably take many singers out of their "comfort zone" at first, but gradually this level of activity will become familiar. This is the level of intensity that they need to employ as performers. Only when the story is fully communicated through the singer's entire physical and mental powers will the message reach and move the audience.

As described in chapter 8, the judging categories for barbershop competitions reward skilled application in all the areas that create a strong performance. Therefore, these category descriptions serve as models or guides for the singers as they work toward becoming consummate barbershop performers.

The variety of exercises or tools that can be used to teach good barbershop singing knows no limit. One of the benefits of having a coach come in is to gain exposure to new tools and new perspectives. Directors can attend a training event and come home energized with a new "bag of tricks" to enliven their rehearsals. But always the goal is the same—to equip each individual singer to be able to make the best possible contribution to the overall unit sound. It is our challenge and our joy.

NOTE

1. H. Wesley Balk, *Performing Power: A New Approach for the Singer-Actor* (Minneapolis: University of Minnesota Press, 1985), 57–78.

BIBLIOGRAPHY

Balk, H. Wesley. *Performing Power: A New Approach for the Singer-Actor.* Minneapolis: University of Minnesota Press, 1985.

Hicks, Val. "Choral Warmups—the Perfect 5th—the Magic Interval." N.p.: Private publication, 1997.

8

STANDARDS FOR BARBERSHOP SINGING

Here Comes the Judge

Almost from the beginning of organized barbershop singing, performers have competed with their fellow singers for recognition, awards, and prestige and have freely offered their musical and performance skills to the judgment and criticism of others. Within fourteen months of its formation, SPEBSQSA held its first "National Open" quartet contest in Tulsa, Oklahoma. The rules for this first competition were, by almost any standard, loose. Any quartet of four (male) singers was eligible to compete, and they could sing "two songs of their choosing" with or without accompaniment. Winners were to be called world champions, with second and third place finishers to be given somewhat less-exalted titles. The judges were local dignitaries, educators, and politicians. Twenty-three foursomes from as far away as Illinois competed, and at the end of the contest, the Bartlesville Barflies from nearby Bartlesville, Oklahoma, were named champions. For the first ten years of competition, the rules changed every year. In 1951, SPEBSQSA leaders settled on a set of contest rules that served for the next two decades. Since then, there have been two complete rewrites, one in the early 1970s and another in 1992. The 1992 revision is the system (with some minor changes over time) under which contests are held today. ♪

In the early days, barbershop chapter meetings always contained informal group singing, as well as opportunities to separate into quartets.

The fun of singing together as a larger ensemble led to the creation of more formal "choruses," which in turn spurred a movement to add choruses to the contests. In 1953, the first international chorus competition was held, with the Great Lakes Chorus of Grand Rapids, Michigan, named as champions. Today, choruses provide the method by which most barbershoppers participate in the hobby, and a chorus competition is an integral part of almost every convention. ♪

Currently, contests are staffed by one to five judges per scoring category; these judges are rigorously trained and certified every three years. Every judge awards each song performed a point value of 0 to 100 points. The Barbershop Harmony Society (BHS) website contains a condensed description of each scoring category and a downloadable version of the complete *Contest & Judging Manual*. Here are "unofficial" capsule descriptions of each category:

The Music Category. A *music judge* evaluates the song and arrangement as performed. Without reference to the written arrangement, as the performance progresses, he or she (in 2016 the BHS opened its judging program to qualified females) evaluates the quality and appropriateness of the musical elements in the song and arrangement, together with the level of musical artistry demonstrated by the performer. To arrive at a final score for each song performed, the judge factors in the degree to which the elements of the song—its rhythmic components, its mood or story, its lyrical content—are supported and, finally, assesses the amount of consonant harmony present in the performance.

The Performance Category. A *performance judge* evaluates how effectively the performers bring the song to life. He or she adjudicates the dramatic, vocal, and physical skills the performer employs to meld the musical and emotional elements of the performance into a unified, entertaining whole. Ultimately, the judge arrives at a score for each song that reflects the degree to which the performer communicates with and entertains the audience during the ensemble's complete time onstage, including the time before, between, and after each song is presented.

The Singing Category. A *singing judge* evaluates artistic singing in the barbershop style. A hallmark of the style is the "lock and ring" achieved when each singer employs precise intonation, a unified approach to vocal production, uniform vowel sounds, and a specific approach to the relative volume level of each part in the chord. When the presence of this "barbershop sound" is supported by a freely produced, resonant vocal tone, an artistic approach to the musical line, a clear communication of the emotion of the lyrics, and a high degree of synchrony throughout the performance, a high singing-category score is achieved.

The structure of the BHS competition system revolves around its seventeen districts. Each district, and in some cases smaller geographic units called *divisions*, holds one or more contests each year to select youth quartet champions, senior quartet champions, district quartet and chorus champions, and qualifiers to advance to the international level. In some cases, a qualifying score is used, and every competitor who achieves it qualifies for advancement to the next level. In other cases, simply besting all the other competitors at a particular contest—usually earning the title "champion"—qualifies the group for the international level.

Shortly after the formation of the women's first—and still major—barbershop harmony group, Sweet Adelines International (SAI), the ladies began to hold contests, too. And this, of course, required judges and judging criteria. Two years after its founding in 1945, the organization had created a system for choosing the best women's barbershop quartet in the nation, and they crowned the Decaturettes as the first "Queens of Harmony" in Tulsa, Oklahoma. ♪

In 1973, a chorus competition was held along with the international quartet contest, and the first international chorus champion was the

Figure 8.1. The Decaturettes. *Courtesy of Sweet Adelines International*

Racine Chorus of Racine, Wisconsin. Over the years, the system and its training programs have been refined and revised, and today a very thorough process exists for selecting, training, and certifying judges in four categories: sound, music, expression, and showmanship. ♪

The Sweet Adelines International *Judging Category Description Book* delineates the following descriptions of the four categories:

The Sound Category. "The focus of the sound category is the evaluation of unit sound in the barbershop style. Unit sound occurs when tones are properly produced, accurately tuned, blended and balanced. In barbershop harmony, this is referred to as 'lock-and-ring.' Although the sound judge does not evaluate vocal technique in and of itself, the sound category does include evaluation of the basics of correct singing."[1] The components that, combined, result in the locked, ringing, unit sound are good vocal production, accuracy of both horizontal individual part lines and vertical parts within individual chords, blended vocal qualities, cone-shaped balance of voices and sections (bass voice strongest to set up the overtone series), and overall application of vocal and stylistic technique that enhances the identifiable characteristics of the barbershop style.[2]

The Music Category. "The primary focus of the music category is the performance of a song arranged in four-part harmony, barbershop style. The music judge evaluates the musicality of the performance, the quality of the song and arrangement and the adherence of the performing ensemble to the barbershop style. She awards a performance wherein: the song and arrangement are accurately performed and within the vocal capabilities of the performer; the musical performance is appropriate to the lyrics, to the harmonic and rhythmic content and to our accepted standards of musical artistry; the song is lyrically and melodically appropriate to the barbershop art form and has been arranged with harmonization and voicing consistent with the characteristics of the barbershop style. . . . The extent to which a song adheres to the barbershop style is determined by the following characteristics unique to this form of music: chord structure, arrangement, the cone-shaped sound, untempered tuning, delivery and interpretation. These are integral factors which contribute to the 'lock-and-ring' characteristic of singing in the barbershop style."[3]

The Expression Category. "The focus of the expression category is the evaluation of the performer's ability to communicate musically.

In vocal music, communication is strengthened by the meaningful delivery of lyrics, musical diction, artistic phrasing, appropriate dynamics and a projection of sincere emotion."[4] The components of the expression category include reasonable proficiency in the basics of good vocal production; reasonable proficiency in the vertical synchronization of all elements of the song, including production of vowels, injection of consonants, turning of diphthongs, attack and release of all syllables, and use of nuances and vocal inflections so that the lyrical presentation demonstrates absolute unity; techniques of phrasing, tempo and rhythm used effectively to support the subtler elements of inflection, finesse and smooth delivery of the words so that the result is a sensitive, artistic, musical presentation.[5]

The Showmanship Category. "The focus of the showmanship category is the evaluation of the salesmanship of the musical product. This includes the elements of preparation, the visual plan and the creation and communication of on-stage magic. With effective showmanship, the performer is able to enhance what the listener hears by reinforcing it with what the viewer sees, creating a total performance. Showmanship is an intangible art, affected neither by age nor by beauty. With showmanship, a little talent can seem great; without showmanship, the greatest talent can be lost." The showmanship judge awards a performance wherein "thorough advance attention has been given to all details of preparation, so that no visual or musical flaw creates such a distraction that the impact of the total performance is weakened; an appropriate mood is established and the performer appears so relaxed, poised and self-assured that the audience is readily able to respond to that mood; the separate musical and visual facets of the performance enhance and support each other, combining to create a total, entertaining performance."[6]

SAI has recently added an "open" division at the regional level. This allows a quartet or chorus to compete for score and evaluation but does not allow them to qualify for a higher level of competition. There are no "winners" in open division contests; each competitor is assigned a level. This allows competitors not wishing to compete at the international level to receive help with their entertainment skills, aiding them in honing their product for their audiences at home.

For many years, SAI has required an "entertainment package" of their chorus competitors who reach the finals at the international level.

This lengthier presentation allows the competitors to hone their skills at performing highly polished packages to entertain audiences throughout the year.

Harmony, Inc., also holds area and international chorus and quartet competitions, and they have traditionally patterned their judging system after that of the BHS. In fact, they have sent their judges to be trained at the men's judging schools and often use BHS judges for their contests. Their international quartet champions are crowned "Harmony Queens." ♪

After the contest is over, the quartets and choruses have a lot of information to ponder. The judges' comments are copious and specific; there are many things to work on to garner the improvement the ensemble wants and needs. The first meeting after the competition is usually devoted to reviewing the judges' comments and discussing the ways in which the ensemble can best make use of the recommendations for improvement. Priorities must be assigned to help organize and focus the work ahead—and of course, this all needs to be folded into the regular events of chorus or quartet life: new songs to learn, repertoire to be maintained, general skills to be honed, fun to be had. Often, though, to make sure the learning achieved at the contest site is not lost, a three- or perhaps six-month plan will be created. This will identify the main areas of improvement to be addressed, together with specific exercises, drills, and instruction to be incorporated into the rehearsal schedule to achieve that improvement. Often a specific coach is invited to visit the chapter with the goal of working on a particular skill or group of skills: vocal production, intonation maintenance, emotion and physical involvement in the delivery of songs, general musicality issues, and so forth. The principal aim, of course, is to use the information gained at the contest site to ensure that the performance level of the ensemble is in fact elevated, resulting in a more satisfying experience for the performers and a better product for their audiences.

Barbershoppers love their competitions and work long and hard to present their best performances on the contest stage. They wear their medals and their crowns with great pride. However, there is also a great spirit of support and cooperation among the competing groups. Everyone wants everyone else to sing well and to succeed. It is typical that when a quartet or chorus enters the audience after having competed,

Figure 8.2. For Heaven's Sake Quartet. *Courtesy of Betsy Groner Photography*

they are welcomed with enthusiastic applause. Barbershop singers love to compete because it challenges them to strive for the very highest standards in the performance of their unique and exciting art form. Whether or not they win awards, they are educated through the comments of the judges, who share with them the ways that they can continue to improve their performance. And at international-level contests, they see and hear the very best singers from all over the globe. Singers come away from competition with fresh enthusiasm, determined to work even harder to lock and ring those chords!

NOTES

1. Sweet Adelines International (SAI), *Judging Category Description Book*, II-B-1.
2. SAI, *Judging Category Description Book*, II-A-1.
3. SAI, *Judging Category Description Book*, II-D-1.
4. SAI, *Judging Category Description Book*, II-D-1.
5. SAI, *Judging Category Description Book*, II-D-1.
6. SAI, *Judging Category Description Book*, II-C-1.

BIBLIOGRAPHY

Sweet Adelines International. *Judging Category Description Book*. Tulsa, OK: Sweet Adelines International, 1989.

9

BECOMING A BETTER BARBERSHOPPER

Education in the Craft

If there is one thing barbershoppers enjoy almost as much as singing barbershop, it is learning how to sing *better* barbershop. This emphasis on education is clearly reflected in the literature of the various organizations. The mission statement of Sweet Adelines International (SAI) declares that "Sweet Adelines International is a highly respected worldwide organization of women singers committed to advancing the musical art form of barbershop harmony through education and performances."[1] The website of Harmony, Inc. (HI), proclaims that "Harmony, Inc. is an international, non-profit organization whose purpose is to empower all women through education, friendship and a cappella singing in the barbershop style."[2]

In their "Vision & Mission," the Barbershop Harmony Society (BHS) states: "Our district and international conventions, festivals, and educational conferences incorporate contests, activities, and training sessions to meet the needs of our membership and their families. We continually strive for improvement in individual, quartet, chorus, and Society activities, performances, and events."[3]

Barbershoppers of all levels are aware that we can continue to improve our performances, and we also understand that any organization that does not constantly recruit and train new members is doomed to pass into oblivion.

COACHING

The most popular and probably the most effective educational tool in the barbershop world is the practice of coaching. Coaching is not organized in any formal way beyond the keeping of lists of qualified coaches that interested singers can draw on. Barbershop groups are in the habit of inviting an outside expert to coach them in singing and performing skills. Even the smallest choruses with limited financial resources will often build into their budgets the funds to bring in a coach once or twice a year. A chorus headed for competition may invite coaches to come even more often. Many regions or districts offer financial assistance to help choruses defray the cost of bringing in a coach.

There are several advantages to receiving coaching over attending a training school. First, because the coach comes to the group, coaching reaches almost every chorus member, not just those who have the time and money to travel. Second, coaching is personalized, so the training directly addresses the needs of individual singers, as well as the specific group. Third, a chorus can select a coach who specializes in the exact skills the chorus wants to work on at a particular time. Fourth, coaching shares ideas, skills, and techniques that the local director can adopt and reinforce on a weekly basis.

Because ideas are so willingly and freely shared through the experience of coaching, there is a wonderful, open spirit in our organizations. We are one for all and all for one. Everyone wants everyone to become better singers. It is not at all uncommon for a coach to be helping a chorus that will be his or her competitor in an upcoming contest. Competitions are loving, supportive events, where all rejoice in the success of others and thrill to the achievement of high-caliber barbershop singing.

Quartets are also eager for coaching. Often part of a chorus's coaching weekend includes time for the coach to work with several of the local quartets. Sometimes a quartet will make arrangements to coach with someone when they are all attending a regional school. Or a quartet and a coach may drive some distance to work together.

Of course, in this day of ever-more-sophisticated technology, many choruses and quartets are taking advantage of the opportunity to be coached electronically via software such as Skype or FaceTime. Though electronic coaching may not be quite as effective as in-person interaction, it can certainly be a fine supplement in one's overall coaching experience.

So you may wonder, who are these amazing coaches who are hired to work with our barbershop ensembles? Because coaching is not a formalized program, there are no official qualifications for determining who can coach. A coach may be the director of an international- or regional-winning chorus or a member of a high-scoring or champion quartet. A coach may be the person in your chorus who is a local voice or dance teacher. Simply put, a coach can be any person who knows something you want or need to learn and is willing to share that knowledge with you, either for money or free of charge. A few people in the barbershop world are in such demand as coaches that they have given up their day jobs and gone to coaching full time. Most coaches, however, do this work part time. Some coaches who are professional musicians consider their coaching as an extension of their professional work. Others who work outside of music consider their coaching as a side job that brings them a little spending money, which they may turn around and spend on their barbershop hobby.

The most inspiring thing about coaching is that no groups—not even international-champion choruses or quartets—think they are too good or too important to get coaching. In fact, it seems the more skilled a group gets, the more they want to be coached so they can continue to improve. This is a great reminder to all of us that we never reach the point where we know everything about our art. There is always room for learning, growth, and improvement. In this regard, the barbershop organizations are a powerful role model for music ensembles the world over.

PERSONAL VOCAL INSTRUCTION

As the barbershop organizations have grown in their understanding of good vocal production, it has become clear that one of the best ways to help people sing better is through personal vocal instruction (PVI), known in the world at large as the private voice lesson. Barbershoppers are eager to have PVIs at every opportunity. Sometimes a coach is invited to spend a weekend with a chorus, giving PVIs to individual singers for the entire time. Other times, a coach may work with the chorus on Friday and Saturday and conduct PVIs on Sunday. Opportunities for PVIs are often provided at regional education events, or a chorus may invite a coach to come to a weekly chorus rehearsal and give PVIs, with individual singers slipping out of rehearsal for a brief time. PVIs may be given in pairs to help singers with the cost or with the nerves that can come when singing alone in front of a coach or teacher. PVIs usually last a half hour or an hour. The hope is that each singer will receive one or two new tools based on his or her own personal vocal needs that he or she can use to help improve his or her singing.

Who teaches PVIs? Once again, since this is not a formal program; anyone can teach a PVI. Perhaps a chorus director will give PVIs to her chorus members, or a chorus section leader may give PVIs to his section members. Quartet members may give PVIs to each other. Perhaps ideally, one should get a PVI from a professional voice teacher trained in the fine points of vocal production. There are many professional voice teachers in our barbershop organizations. It would also be an ideal opportunity for National Association of Teachers of Singing (NATS) members or other professional voice teachers to provide this service for the barbershop groups in their local communities. If the voice teacher is prepared and willing to teach the techniques of contemporary commercial music (CCM)—that is, pop-style music—the barbershop groups will welcome their offers of assistance. Voice teachers can check the websites of the Barbershop Harmony Society, Sweet Adelines International, Harmony, Inc., or any of the several international barbershop organizations for listings of the choruses in their localities.

Technology also has a part to play in facilitating PVIs. It is easier to give a PVI electronically than to coach a larger group of people online. And working online can enable the singer to get a PVI from the teacher of his or her choice, even though they may live many miles apart. Undoubtedly, there will be more online PVI work as technology continues to be upgraded and refined.

Again, the goal of getting a PVI is to have that valuable extra pair of eyes and ears to observe one's singing and give feedback and encouragement to the singer. The PVI enables the singer to feel more confident about working on his or her own individual singing skills and making a better contribution to his or her chorus or quartet.

DISTRICT/REGIONAL/AREA SCHOOLS

Each district (BHS), region (SAI), and area (HI) of our barbershop organizations has the responsibility of providing educational opportunities for the members of that area. Members of choruses pay dues to their organizations, and a portion of these funds is allocated regionally and internationally to help support educational opportunities—a great investment!

A district may have several educational events each year. Often a guest faculty member or champion quartet is brought in as the leader for the event. In fact, almost every BHS district school has a past international champion quartet as part of its faculty. Other times, regional leaders serve as faculty for various classes. Sometimes the participants are assigned to special choruses for the weekend and have the opportunity to sing with a chorus or director different from their own. Since most of our choruses are small (fifteen to forty members), it can be a thrill for a small chorus member to sing with a larger ensemble. Also, there is much to be learned from singing under a chorus director different from one's own.

A district school may have a central theme and offer classes related to that theme or simply offer a variety of classes related to the craft of barbershop singing. If there is a guest faculty member, usually all participants attend that person's classes. If faculty are local, there may be choices of classes to attend. Classes may cover a large variety of topics, for example: directing skills, coaching skills, arranging skills, song writing, music theory, vocal techniques, voice-part-specific skills, quartet skills, section-leader training, tag singing, woodshedding, choreography, team building, management skills, grant writing, stress management, emcee skills, long-range planning, communication skills, chapter management, membership recruitment, and many more. Area meetings give members a chance to see their friends, appreciate and learn from a variety of organizational leaders, and develop a greater sense of the scope of our worldwide organizations. Almost every singer who attends a regional event wants to return again and again.

INTERNATIONAL SCHOOLS

For several decades, the Barbershop Harmony Society has operated its largest training school, Harmony University, held for many years during the summer at Missouri Western State University in St. Joseph, Missouri, and now in residence at Belmont University in Nashville, Tennessee. All directors in the organization are encouraged to attend the

Directors College, which is a major component of this event, and some scholarships are offered to assist directors in this effort. The top faculty of the Society teach the classes at Harmony University, and the offerings are extensive. The school is broken into four "colleges": Harmony College for general instruction in the barbershop craft; Directors College, with courses and seminars of interest to barbershop chorus directors; Music Educators College, with offerings of special interest to music teachers; and Quartet College, which offers coaching and general sessions to help quartets improve their performances. Harmony University is open to all and offers many opportunities to learn, grow, and sing in groups large and small, bond with other musicians who love this style of music, and make new friendships and invigorate existing ones.

From 1999 to 2008, Sweet Adelines International held its International Education Symposium either at Trinity College in San Antonio, Texas, or at Furman University in Greenville, South Carolina. Staffed by SAI international faculty, tracks of classes were taught in a wide variety of subjects—something to please every chorus member and leader. The organization has recently offered a summer education event titled "A Cappella Harmony Academy" (AHA), which offered training for directors and other chorus leaders. In 2016, AHA was held in Auckland, New Zealand. By popular demand, the organization will resume holding the International Education Symposium in the summer of 2017.

INTERNET EDUCATIONAL OFFERINGS

Barbershop organizations have embraced the advantages of modern technology. Webinars and online classes are regularly offered in many subject areas, and no doubt these courses will continue to increase as technology becomes more sophisticated. Also, course handouts and other educational resources are available to members on the organizations' websites.

SPECIALIZED TRAINING: DIRECTORS, JUDGES, AND ARRANGERS

Certain jobs in the barbershop world require highly specialized skills, and the organizations offer schools and training programs to meet these needs. Directors, judges, and arrangers are among those who attend these special sessions. In all three organizations, there is a strong emphasis on education for chorus directors, as organizational leaders believe that the chorus director is the most influential person in the life of the average barbershopper and that the life and spirit of the organization is modeled by and transmitted through the director.

Director Training

The Barbershop Harmony Society has long placed emphasis on the training of directors. It is understood that since most barbershoppers get their musical experience as members of a chorus, the director of that chorus plays a uniquely important role in the quality of the members' experience. Training in chorus directing is multifaceted, and to guarantee the members of his or her chapter the most return on their investment in time at the meetings each week, the director must seek continual improvement. Conducting skills, teaching methods, voice pedagogy, song-selection criteria, sound-management skills, music theory, rehearsal planning, leadership, and many other aspects of directing a successful chorus are taught every summer at Harmony University (HU), and variations of many of these classes are also offered at district schools. The job of a chorus director is not an easy one, and recognizing his or her importance to the success of a chapter, scholarships are available for frontline directors to HU. Many chapter leaders budget for the expenses of such classes for their director each year as well. It's hard to think of a better use of a chapter's funds.

Sweet Adelines International's primary education program for directors is the Director Certification Program (DCP). The DCP is a home-study program designed to provide current and potential directors with the information they need to be successful in their jobs. The program is composed of eleven study modules: (1) Directing Skills, (2) Analytical Listening, (3) Organizational Knowledge & Director Resources, (4) Teaching Skills, (5) Management Skills, (6) Judging Categories & Competition, (7) Vocal Production, (8) Communication Skills, (9) Music Theory, (10) Rehearsal Planning & Implementation, and (11) Chorus Performance. Under the guidance of the regional DCP coordinator, the participant studies at home and, when ready, takes written tests or undergoes evaluations by designated personnel. When satisfactory scores have been attained in all modules, the participant reaches the level of certified director. There are three other levels that are obtained by frontline directors in competitions: Harmony 500 director (directors whose choruses score at least 500 points), master director (600 points), and master director 700 (700 points). (The maximum regional contest score is 800 points.) Other chorus music leaders are also encouraged to study the DCP modules to avail themselves of the knowledge available to help them do their jobs.

In addition to the DCP, SAI provides frequent director-training classes and workshops at regional and international events, such as the International Education Symposium (IES). The IES has a directors' track, which provides classes in many of the above-mentioned topics and features an outstanding guest faculty member who is a widely known, nationally successful choral director.

Harmony, Inc., hosted a specialized school for directors' training for many years but recently shifted its strategy to leverage the resources offered by the Barbershop Harmony Society at their annual Harmony University event. Having turned to the brother organization for fulfillment of the training itself, Harmony, Inc., focuses instead on its Directors First fund-raising campaign. Directors First is a program designed to raise funds from among the Harmony, Inc., membership and supporters to send a dozen directors per year to Harmony University. The success of this program means that one musical director or other musical leader from each chapter will attend the intensive, week-long Harmony University within a window of five years. This rotation is a strategy the organization believes will be far more successful than hosting its own training schools, which were often shorter in length and more limited in scope of skill building.

In addition to removing the financial obstacle of attending Harmony University by providing full scholarships to Harmony, Inc., directors, the Directors First program also empowers each chapter in Harmony, Inc., to determine its area of greatest need when it comes to musical leadership. While some chapters opt to give their slot to frontline musical directors, others have strong directors and prefer to strengthen their secondary tier of musical leadership, such as assistant directors or section leaders.[4]

Judge Training

All certified contest judges in the Barbershop Harmony Society undergo an extensive vetting and practice period before being certified.

After certification, every judge is required to attend a three-day school, called Category Training School, every three years to be recertified. At this school, many hours are spent scoring and making notes on video performances. All the scores for each performance are compared, and extensive statistical analysis is performed to help each judge align his scoring levels with his peers. This process produces a body of certified judges who have proven their ability to accurately and fairly score performances by all groups at all contests. The second major component of Category School is training in the important work of meeting with contestants following the contest to explain the scoring they received and offer them coaching and other help to improve their future performances.

What does it take to be a judge? Judges in the music, performance, or singing categories have a strong desire to help contestants—both choruses and quartets—achieve improvement. Judges must be experienced barbershoppers with a proven record of success as singers, musicians, and performers and also have demonstrable skills as coaches and teachers of barbershop. Significant experience as a participant in barbershop competitions is a must. It is also desirable that a judge have musical experience outside the barbershop world—for example, arranging music, teaching voice, or working in theater. According to the Society Contest & Judging Committee (SCJC), "[The committee] is looking for people who can quickly evaluate a performance, assess strengths and weaknesses, and provide instructive feedback within a short period of time."[5]

Sweet Adelines International has a very intensive and rigorous training program for its judges. An interested person begins by filling out an application and specifying the category in which she would like to judge: sound, music, expression, or showmanship. If she is accepted as an applicant, she is required to take two written tests—one in general knowledge and one specific to her judging category. If she passes the tests, she is asked to trial score a regional competition. Her scores and comments are compared to those of the official judge in her category, and the Judge Specialist Committee (which includes a specialist in each category, as well as a moderator) analyzes whether or not she has demonstrated above-average skill for judging and writing commentary. If she is deemed to have potential as a judge, she is accepted as an approved candidate judge (ACJ). After becoming an ACJ, the candidate is invited to attend an ACJ workshop sponsored by Sweet Adelines International, which is held in conjunction with a regional contest. At this workshop, the ACJ works closely with the judge specialist in her category to perfect her skills. From this point on, she continues the trial-scoring process in order to learn her craft. After each contest, the ACJ receives critiques on her work so that she can continue to learn and upgrade her skills. As a trial scorer, she participates in the discussions and the watching of preliminary videos that prepare the official judges for their task of judging. The candidate judge receives a yearly evaluation by her analyst, and if she maintains high-enough scores, she continues in the program. She continues in the trial-scoring process for an indefinite length of time until it is determined that her scores and comments are at the appropriate level to serve on a panel. It typically takes several years to accomplish this step. To advance to the next level, she will be asked to write an essay that includes details about her category, as well as a full description of the way the four categories relate to each other. If her essay is accepted, she becomes an approved judge. She will continue judging regionally until she is ready for the final advancement. Once she has successfully judged for a number of years and demonstrated that she has the consistency and accuracy required, she will be advanced to the certified level. A certified judge can judge at the international contest, and she is eligible to attend any judge-training opportunities sponsored by Sweet Adelines International.[6]

Harmony, Inc., trains and certifies judges in four categories: music, performance, singing, and chairman of judges. Formal training is held annually in January at HI's Category Training School, but informal training is ongoing through the guidance of category directors. Certification, requiring many years of training, is granted only after a candidate has demonstrated the skills necessary to consistently score and evaluate contest performances within the HI guidelines.

Areas of competency used for certification include category knowledge, communication skills, evaluation/teaching skills, interpersonal skills, and scoring ability.

Qualification Area #1—*Category Knowledge:* Identify appropriate events within a performance that contribute to, or detract from, effective performance in that category.

Qualification Area #2—*Communication Skills:* Communicate category concepts effectively, using appropriate verbal and nonverbal skills, resulting in performers receiving a clear understanding of relevant category information.

Qualification Area #3—*Evaluation/Communication/Teaching Skill:*
1. Convey key strengths and weaknesses of a performance supported by appropriate examples from a given performance.
2. Assist performers by recommending appropriate changes in their performance or rehearsal techniques.

HI area conventions and contests (for choruses and quartets) are sponsored mid-April to mid-June and serve as qualifying rounds for the annual international convention and contests, held in early November. Area contests are judged by a double panel—meaning two judges per category—and the international contest by a triple panel of judges.

Judging panels are supplemented by certified judges from the Barbershop Harmony Society. HI judges serve on at least two contest panels each year. Following the scoring of performances, they provide coaching evaluations for all choruses and quartets at the area contests.[7]

Arranger Training

Sweet Adelines International is currently studying ways to improve training for arrangers. Some regions in SAI have an arrangers coordinator, whose job it is to discover potential arrangers and to provide arranger education at the regional level. If there is no such coordinator in place, then a regional education coordinator can put a prospective arranger in touch with someone who can assist her in her quest. Persons who succeed as barbershop arrangers must possess a strong knowledge of music theory and must be willing to study in a disciplined manner to learn the specific skills of arranging in the barbershop genre. Many a budding arranger has heard these words from her mentor: "That's beautiful, but it's not barbershop." Once a potential arranger has taken some regional classes and has studied the SAI *Arrangers Manual*, she may be taken under the wing of a mentor (usually a certified or master music arranger), who will critique her work and help her advance in her skills. When she has reached a high-enough skill level and shows strong promise, she may be nominated for the Sweet Adelines International Music Arrangers Program (IMAP). IMAP is a two-year scholarship program that awards five scholarships at a time, providing funding for the candidate to study intensively with a mentor and continue to grow in barbershop-arranging skills. The IMAP coordinators determine who will receive scholarships and examine the work of the candidates after one year of study to determine whether they may continue to the second year of the program. At the end of the two years, the IMAP coordinators may advance the candidate to the level of certified music arranger. There is also a higher level of recognition, master music arranger, which is awarded to longtime arrangers who have contributed a large body of successful work to the organization.

Arranger training in BHS is less formal than that of SAI. BHS members who are interested in becoming more skilled at arranging in the barbershop style will find many manuals from the Society and myriad courses at the district and international level to help them with that task. Arrangers who are interested in becoming more skilled will hone their craft simply by arranging and by consulting with more-experienced arrangers when needed. The aspiring arranger will usually begin by creating works for his own quartet. As his skills improve and his work is exposed to others through show and contest appearances, he may be asked to share his work—or create something new—for other groups. Eventually, the most talented and creative arrangers find that their fame has spread, and the best of these will eventually become known to barbershoppers worldwide. All of the top BHS arrangers—most of whom arrange for both men's and women's voicings—have websites that list arrangements for sale, often accompanied by four-part learning tracks. A quick search for "barbershop arrangers" in your favorite Internet search engine will provide a plethora of highly skilled arrangers of both genders, together with lists of their available work.

CONVENTIONS AND COMPETITIONS

As we discussed in chapter 7, competition at the regional and international level is very important in the barbershop world, and it certainly can be said that these events are among our most important educational vehicles. Attending a chorus or quartet contest enables singers to hear a wide range of barbershop-singing skill levels and to be exposed to role-model examples of our art form. We see and hear singers putting their best foot forward and delivering the strongest vocal performances of which they are capable. Less-skilled singers cannot help but be inspired by the performances of the regional top medalists, both choruses and quartets, and our international competitions allow us to see and hear barbershop singing at its very finest—the goal to which we all aspire. Fortunately, our international contests and many of our district and regional contests are now available as live (and sometimes archived) webcasts, so the folks back home—both the families of competitors and singers unable to travel to the venues—are able to enjoy the results of all those months of work. Truly technology is assisting us mightily in our efforts to bring barbershop harmony all around the world.

At the regional level, competitors in Sweet Adelines contests receive written comments on their scoring sheets from the judges. Following Barbershop Harmony Society and Harmony, Inc., competitions, contestants are given the opportunity to meet with judges from each category to receive feedback, coaching, and guidance that can lead to additional success in future contests.

Since large numbers of barbershoppers gather to compete and to cheer on their favorite competitors at international competitions, all the organizations take advantage of this chance to offer educational opportunities to their members. Master classes are conducted by the reigning-champion choruses and quartets, and additional classes are offered during the week, as convention time permits. According to Christina Lewellen, HI's international president, Harmony, Inc., provides more than twenty hours of education offerings each year at their International Convention and Contests.[8]

Competitors receive written comments on their scoring sheets from the judges, but no oral evaluations are given at the international level due to time constraints. Contestants are encouraged to follow up with the judges by e-mail or phone if they wish to discuss the judges' comments in greater detail.

HARMONY BRIGADES

Some barbershop singers just cannot get enough opportunities to sing this exciting four-part a cappella music, and this is especially true of some of the more skilled singers who love a musical challenge. Some members of the Barbershop Harmony Society held the first harmony brigade in Fort Morgan, Alabama, in 1958.[9] Now brigades are held all around North America, and a manual is published to facilitate the organizing of these events. The *Operations Manual* makes clear the purpose of a brigade: "Brigade is an invitational for good quartet-level singers that provides a high-quality, eXtreme Quartetting weekend for men who are vocally capable, committed to learning challenging arrangements, and who are prepared to enjoy thrilling success in rally activities."[10]

As usual, the women were not content to let the men have all the fun, so they organized their own Women's Harmony Brigade on the East Coast in 2014. Women's brigade coordinator Jennifer Newman explains that the brigade is designed to "fill a niche by providing high level, experienced quartet singers the opportunity to learn challenging repertory on their own and come together for a weekend of singing in limitless quartet combinations."[11] Newman also explained that "the Women's Harmony Brigade has always been an independent organization, open to any female who loves to sing barbershop in quartet formation. We have participants from SAI, HI, female affiliate members of BHS, and women whose only barbershop fix is our annual event."[12]

Al Bonney, veteran of several men's brigades, describes his experience this way: "The Brigade experience was fun and interesting to me for several reasons: musical challenge (to sing tougher arrangements) and fellowship (making new barbershop friends) being among the top. The most meaningful reason, however, was being able to participate at a musical level considerably above that normally available to me. Being able to flex my musical muscles making really good music and hearing myself in a big chorus and quartet ringing many of the chords added considerable joy to my everyday chorus musical experience in my hometown chorus."[13]

The brigade experience has also reached overseas to Germany, Sweden, and the United Kingdom, with doubtless more countries to follow. In addition, a miniversion of the Harmony Brigade, called Harmony Platoon, is held at many of the conventions of the Barbershop Harmony Society. Men can participate without having to make a special trip to a location, and they learn four or five songs instead of eleven or twelve, but the thrill is just the same.

TRAVEL OPPORTUNITIES

Using a format similar to the brigade, where one prepares music individually and assembles at a designated location for a joint-ensemble experience, more and more groups are combining the joys of traveling to exotic locations and singing barbershop. Since 1998, Patsy Meiser, a long-time member of Sweet Adelines, has been taking her Tropical Harmony Chorus to different countries of the world as ambassadors for barbershop harmony. Thus far, the group, composed of women barbershop singers from many locations, has traveled to Austria, Canada, China, England, France, Germany, Greece, Ireland, Italy, and South Africa. On the South Africa trip in 2016, the chorus sponsored a choral workshop attended by six South African choirs, and these groups enjoyed being coached on their own repertory as well as being introduced to barbershop harmony.

Several barbershop groups have participated in cruises with barbershop-singing opportunities, such as Harmony in Hawaii in 2008, following the Sweet Adelines convention in Honolulu. It seems that barbershoppers cannot get enough opportunities to sing and to share their special brand of harmony with the world.

YOUTH PROGRAMS

It is often said that every organization is only one generation away from extinction. Barbershop organizations are no exception, and we understand the importance of teaching the next generation to appreciate and enjoy our beloved art form. We also appreciate the energy, zest, enthusiasm, and fresh ideas that youthful singers bring to our groups. To this end, we encourage choruses to engage and support youth members, sometimes even elementary-aged children (who are often "barbershop brats"). Each organization has also developed formal programs to introduce young singers to barbershop. ♪

The Barbershop Harmony Society sponsors Youth in Harmony, Sweet Adelines International sponsors Young Women in Harmony, and Harmony, Inc., sponsors Harmony for Young Women. The groups sponsor Harmony Explosion and other youth music camps in their various districts. BHS holds a Youth Chorus Festival each year at its midwinter

Figure 9.1.   Open the Doors Youth Chorus. *Courtesy of Lorin May*

international convention. There is also a Collegiate Quartet Competition at their annual July convention, and some of the winners of this contest have gone on to become international quartet champions of the society. Sweet Adelines sponsors the Rising Star Quartet Contest, and the winners of this competition perform at the organization's international convention, as well as on other important occasions. One of the Rising Star champion quartets has gone on to become Sweet Adelines International Queens of Harmony. Harmony, Inc., sponsors a showcase chorus named the Minor Chords, which performs annually at their international convention.

Harmony Foundation International (BHS) and the Young Singers Foundation (SAI) have been established to provide ongoing funding for youth programs and music scholarships. Harmony, Inc., also provides music scholarships for youth members and students pursuing music degrees.

REACHING OUT TO MUSIC EDUCATORS

The barbershop organizations are doing more than ever before to reach out to music educators. For many years, the National Association for

Music Education (NAfME) has presented the NAfME Award to a Sweet Adeline and NAfME member who has made outstanding contributions in her field and who has successfully incorporated barbershop singing into her school curriculum. Beginning in 2016, a similar award will be presented to a Sweet Adeline by the Canadian Music Educators' Association.

Also for many years, the Barbershop Harmony Society has offered scholarships and a special course track for music educators at Harmony University to introduce music teachers to barbershop and provide tools to help them incorporate barbershop singing into their school curriculum. The BHS continues to work with the American Choral Directors Association (ACDA) and NAfME to find ways to encourage singing at all levels for all students in the schools. In the recent past, the Society has featured its best choruses and quartets in "showcase concerts" at NAfME in-service conferences, and Crossroads, the BHS 2009 International Champion Quartet, was honored in 2016 with NAfME's Stand for Music Award and was featured at the Hill Day collegiate summit in Washington, DC.

This book, *So You Want to Sing Barbershop*, is itself a conversation between barbershop organizations and the National Association of Teachers of Singing. Encouraging people to enjoy singing beautiful music benefits us all, and the more we can cooperate to make it happen, the better our world will be. Education in the craft is one of the most important benefits that a singer enjoys as a barbershopper. Recordings of barbershop singing through the decades attest to the success of our educational efforts, and the best is yet to come! ♪

NOTES

1. Sweet Adelines International website, accessed January 10, 2016, www.sweetadelineintl.org.
2. Harmony, Inc., website, accessed January 10, 2016, www.harmonyinc.org.
3. Barbershop Harmony Society, "Vision & Mission," Barbershop Harmony Society website, accessed January 10, 2016, www.barbershop.org/about-us/vision-a-mission/.
4. Christina Lewellen, personal communication, February 5, 2017.
5. Barbershop Harmony Society, SCJC, "What Does It Take to Be a Judge?"

6. Renée Porzel, personal communication, February 8, 2017.
7. Christina Lewellen, personal communication, February 5, 2017.
8. Christina Lewellen, personal communication, December 5, 2016.
9. Association of eXtreme Quartetting Harmony Brigades, Inc., *Operations Manual* (N.p.: Barbershop Harmony Society, 2011), 7.
10. Association of eXtreme Quartetting, *Operations Manual*, 5.
11. Jennifer Newman, personal communication, November 3, 2015.
12. Jennifer Newman, personal communication, August 21, 2016.
13. Al Bonney, personal communication, November 12, 2015.

BIBLIOGRAPHY

Association of eXtreme Quartetting Harmony Brigades, Inc., *Operations Manual*. N.p.: Barbershop Harmony Society, 2011.
Barbershop Harmony Society, SCJC. "What Does It Take to Be a Judge?"

CONCLUSION

The Barbershop Culture: Hobby or Lifestyle?

Throughout its history, barbershop singing has both embraced and battled with an inherent existential conflict. Is it a hobby to be enjoyed informally—harmonizing with friends for the pure joy of the act itself—or a performing musical style, with all the work required to perfect songs to be performed for others? Four or more guys or gals standing in a circle relishing the sound of each chord, or a larger number of singers onstage showing proficiency in musical and choreographic performance? The answer is, of course, both. But in that answer lies a gentle conflict.

Most choral groups—small or large—exist to perform. Music is chosen, rehearsals are held, flyers are produced, tickets are printed, advertising is done, and a performance is held. Friends, family, and the public come; the ensemble sings. Of course, barbershop choruses do this, too. Most have one or two shows each year that generate needed operational funds through ticket sales and other means. And as we have seen in chapter 7, many ensembles compete, too. But it all began with four guys standing in a close group and making up harmony to a well-known song, purely for the fun of it—for the sheer joy of singing. As Meredith Willson said, "Tasting the holy essence of four individual mechanisms coming into complete agreement." Therein lies the conflict—sing for ourselves or for others? Time has mostly resolved this in favor of performance, but there still exist a fair number of chapters, particularly in the BHS, that relish and fervently maintain the "singing fraternity" side of the hobby. There are even a number of "quartets only" chapters that, as the name implies, don't contain a chorus at all. But every chapter remains fraternal at its core. Even if their goal is to be a highly polished, professional-grade performing ensemble, there remains a sense of fraternity—of family—that is central to the life of every chapter.

To say that barbershoppers are a family is true, literally and figuratively. The bonding that occurs while working to perfect the harmonies and elevate the individual and collective performance skill level that is central to most chapters' mission creates a feeling of family that usually doesn't exist in traditional choral groups. The feeling that comes from successfully making close harmony together, the fraternal and sororal sense that all-male and all-female ensembles generate, the intensity of emotion created by discovering together the deeper meaning of the lyrics—all of this and more create a very special feeling among barbershoppers. The authors have spent many wonderful years singing in and leading traditional choral ensembles and have enjoyed all those experiences, but we have found a feeling of family in our barbershop chapters—male and female—that exists in no other musical group in our experience. There is a bonding there that simply makes brothers and sisters of us all. Part of this is the welcome that you receive when you visit a chapter. Almost without exception, every new face is greeted as a newfound brother or sister. Music is shared, "riser buddies" are assigned, and a genuine warm welcome is extended to all.

Another sign of the value of the barbershop experience lies in the great number of members who join, simply, for "life." Almost every chapter contains members who have been members of the organization for forty, fifty, or even sixty or more years. These pioneers are honored and revered, for in them lies the institutional memory that helps ground us all. Barbershoppers are often real families, too. Fathers, sons, grandsons, mothers, daughters, granddaughters, uncles, aunts, nephews, nieces, cousins—almost all chapters contain multiple family groups of some description.

There are other unique manifestations of the culture of this hobby. Interchapter activities occur with some frequency, building friendships between members of different chapters. Our organizations offer "dual memberships," which allow members to sing with more than one chapter concurrently. Our conventions, held at least annually, offer opportunities to build lifelong friendships with men and women from other parts of the area, the continent, and, indeed, the world. Our youth outreach programs weld us together, old and young alike. We sing "tags" and commonly held repertoire songs with barbershoppers we meet from all over the world. This kind of shared musical experience is a vital part of any convention. Singing is heard in corners, stairwells, parking garages, hotel lobbies, in restaurants and bars—anywhere singers gather—further bolstering the feeling of family that sharing music with friends and soon-to-be-friends creates.

Social media plays an increasing part in building our culture, too. Every form of Internet gathering exists, and as our youth outreach programs succeed, this online presence grows. For many years, there have been e-mail discussion groups of barbershoppers, such as the SING list and the Harmonet list, which foster camaraderie and the sharing of information among singers all over the world. Facebook, Twitter, Snapchat, blogs, Periscope—any Internet medium you can think of has a barbershop presence. There is even a popular Facebook group titled Barbershop B&B CouchSurfing, which provides a place for barbershoppers who are traveling to a city to let this be known in the hope of finding a fellow barbershopper who will offer them a place to stay for a night or two. The fact that people are willing to have perfect strangers stay in their homes is a testament to the camaraderie fostered and enjoyed by our barbershop groups.

Deke Sharon, vocal producer for the *Pitch Perfect* movies and an enthusiastic honorary member of the Barbershop Harmony Society, has been hailed as "the father of contemporary a cappella singing." He states: "Over the past 80 years, barbershop has created a series of aesthetics and techniques that are so informative to any singer. It bridges the classic and the pop world really beautifully. Anyone who is singing any kind of choral music, any kind of pop, is so much better if they learn barbershop."[1]

Sharon talks further about how we can use singing to change lives:

> We know how singing changes our own lives and makes us feel like a whole human being—so we need to make our number one job as singers

to reach other people. To keep this gift to ourselves is selfish. We can't make the singing be about ourselves. We can't make it be about a gold medal, we can't make it be about impressing judges or how much money we're going to get from the ticket sales. No, we need to make it about changing lives. You go up on that stage and you find someone in the audience, someone out there who is hurting, someone out there who last lost someone, someone out there who is alone. Invite them into our family. That's the greatest gift we can give to society.[2]

The culture of barbershop is a major part of what makes singing this music unique. Barbershoppers often say that we join for the music and stay for the friendship. It's a magical hobby that offers a level of satisfaction many of us simply have not found elsewhere. If you decide to try it, and if you've read this far in our book, you probably have, you'll find, literally, a life-changing way to experience music—all your life long! Welcome aboard!

NOTES

1. Deke Sharon, interview with Lorin May, *Harmonizer*, May/June 2016, 13.
2. Sharon, interview with Lorin May, 15.

BIBLIOGRAPHY

Sharon, Deke. Interview with Lorin May. *Harmonizer*, May/June 2016.

GLOSSARY

A Cappella: The act of singing without instrumental accompaniment.

Ad Lib: The style in which a song segment is delivered without strict adherence to the meter; see free style and rubato.

Afterglow: A party held after a barbershop event.

AHSOW: The Ancient and Harmonious Society of Woodshedders, a subsidiary of the Barbershop Harmony Society, dedicated to preserving and encouraging the original form of the barbershop style—that is, harmonizing to a sung melody without a written arrangement; see woodshedding.

Area: The major geographical subdivision of Harmony, Incorporated; see district, region, and international.

Arrangement: The result of molding a song into a form to be sung by an ensemble by choosing a chord for each melody note, selecting voicings to be used for each chord, adding embellishments, an intro, repeated sections, a tag, and so on.

Arrangement Device: A musical feature added to an arrangement to increase its entertainment and musical value; see embellishment.

Arranger: The creator of an arrangement.

Aspirated Attack: The onset of vocal sound characterized by an audible sound of air immediately prior to the creation of tone.

Attack: The onset of vocal sound, usually described as three types: aspirated, glottal, and coordinated (or balanced).

Audiate: To silently "hear" a pitch before singing it.

Balance: The relative volume (loudness) of the voices in an ensemble.

Ballad: A song that has a slow meter as its primary rhythmic pace, whether performed in tempo or free style.

Barbershop Seventh: A barbershop term for a major-minor seventh chord, frequently used as a "color chord," as well as in its traditional role of propelling movement around the circle of fifths.

Barbershop Brat: A barbershop singer who has one or more barbershopper parents.

Barbershop Harmony Society: The first of several organizations formed to promote and preserve barbershop harmony; see Harmony, Incorporated, and Sweet Adelines International.

Barbershop Style: A style of a cappella vocal music characterized by a consonant four-part chord on every melody note, a predominantly homophonic texture, the melody in the second highest part, and harmonic progression that resolves primarily around the circle of fifths.

Barbershop Sound: The unique sound of a barbershop ensemble resulting from many factors, including voicing, tuning, balance, and vocal-quality choices.

Bari: See baritone.

Bari Cherry: A swipe in the baritone part of a barbershop arrangement that moves from the sixth of the chord to the fifth.

Baritone: (1) The middle harmony part in a barbershop quartet; (2) a singer who sings the middle harmony part in a barbershop quartet.

Bass: (1) The lowest harmony part in a quartet; (2) the singer who sings the lowest harmony part in a quartet.

Beat: (1) A metrical pulse that, when combined in recurring patterns of strong and weak beats, defines meter; (2) a pulsation in sound intensity produced by the combination of two or more tones or partials of slightly different frequency, equal to the difference in frequency between any pair of tones.

Bell Chords: An arrangement device that requires each part to initiate a note in a chord in succession, usually in rhythm.

Belting: The vocal sound achieved when the female chest voice or register is taken into the higher range, creating a loud and stable vocal production.

GLOSSARY

Bird's Eye: See fermata.

Bust a Chord: To sing with gusto, energy, and power.

Cascade: An arrangement device that causes a sung unison to spread into a chord without break in the sound; see peel-off.

Chart: See arrangement.

Chapter: The smallest legal unit of all barbershop organizations.

Chestnut: (1) A familiar song; (2) a commonly known barbershop song; see polecat.

Chest Register: See chest voice.

Chest Voice: A kind of vocal production that commonly occurs in the lower range; see chest register.

Chord: Three or more musical tones sounded together.

Chorditorium: A performance event held at conventions, usually after each round of competition.

Chromatic: (1) Notes that are a half step apart; (2) the use of tones that are not a part of the diatonic scale.

Circle of Fifths: (1) A geometrical diagram illustrating the relationships among the major and minor keys; (2) a progression of chords in which the roots of each are a perfect fifth lower than the last.

Climax: The point of maximum emotion in a song.

Close Harmony: See closed voicing.

Closed Voicing: Voicing in which all parts are on consecutive notes of the chord and when the interval from the highest to lowest note is an octave or less; also called *close harmony*.

Coaching: Education obtained from a source external to the ensemble.

Color: Variation in timbre of the vocal sound.

Color Chord: A chord chosen by an arranger for its aural properties rather than its role in advancing harmonic movement.

Combination Tone: In musical acoustics, a tone of different pitch that is heard when two loud tones are sounded simultaneously; its frequency is the difference or sum of the frequencies of the two primary tones or of their multiples; a component of lock and ring.

Comedic: A style of song or performance that focuses on the humorous value of the presentation; it may be generated by the words, performance choices, or both.

Complete Chord: A voicing of a chord that contains all the notes that define the chord.

Coning: A term that refers to the volume balance of a chord wherein each lower voice is louder than the one above.
Consonance: (1) The simultaneous sounding of two or more tones whose frequencies are related as the ratios of small whole numbers, reducing the audible beats to a minimum; (2) a sound that is said to be pleasing.
Consonant: (1) The presence of consonance; (2) generally, any speech sound that is not a vowel.
Construction: The organization of the components of the song (intro, verse, chorus, interlude, tag, etc.); see form.
Contemporary Commercial Music (CCM): Genres of music other than classical, such as barbershop, country, folk, gospel, jazz, music theater, rock and roll, and so on.
Coordinated Attack: The onset of vocal sound characterized by a healthy balance between adducted pressure on the vocal folds and the initiation of airflow; also known as balanced onset.
Crescendo: A gradual increase in volume.
Decrescendo: A gradual decrease in volume.
Diatonic Scale: A scale involving only notes proper to the prevailing key without chromatic alteration.
Difference Tone: A type of combination tone created when two loud tones of different pitch are sounded simultaneously; its frequency is the difference in the frequencies of the two tones or of their multiples; a component of lock and ring.
Diminuendo: A gradual decrease in volume.
Diphthong: The combination of two vowels in a single syllable, usually a primary and a secondary vowel.
Dissonance: The absence of consonance, resulting from the audible beats produced by two or more tones whose frequencies are not closely related.
District: The major geographical subdivision of the Barbershop Harmony Society; see area, region, and international.
Divorced Tone: A tone in a chord that is not adjacent to other tones in the chord.
Divorced Voicing: Voicing in which one or more adjacent notes skip a part of the chord and in which the highest and lowest notes are more than an octave apart.

Dynamics: The use of contrasting volumes in the ensemble.

Echo: A repeat of a short lyrical statement, usually in the harmony parts.

Embellishment: An arrangement device such as swipe, echo, key change, back time, and patter that creates interest in the arrangement.

Energy: The presence of vitality, intensity, liveliness, and so on in the vocal and visual parts of the presentation.

Enharmonic: The relationship between two notes of different names that occupy the same key on a keyboard or the same fret on fretted instruments.

Equal Temperament: A method of tuning that divides the octave into twelve equal half steps, such as is used in tuning pianos.

Everglow: A party after the afterglow; see preglow, afterglow, and glimmer.

Expanded Sound: The acoustical effect of the interaction of voices singing with just intonation, uniform vowels, proper volume relationships, and precision; see lock and ring.

Falsetto: The head register of the singing voice; this term is used most often in referring to male voices.

Fermata: The symbol placed over a note or rest to indicate that it is to be prolonged substantially beyond its normal duration.

Fifth: The fifth scale degree, which, when functioning as a harmony note, should be sung more loudly than the third and flat seventh of the chord to maximize the consonance of its harmonic series with that of the harmonic series of the root.

Fifth Wheel: An unbidden and therefore unwelcome singer who joins a quartet while they are singing.

First Inversion: A chord in which the third of the chord is the lowest tone.

Flat Seventh: The seventh scale degree lowered one half step, which, when functioning as a harmony note, should be sung less loudly than the root and fifth of the chord to minimize the dissonance of its harmonic series with that of the harmonic series of the root and fifth; see seventh.

Float: The act of softly adding a part to a chord.

Flow: The sensation of progress, motion, and orderliness of the vocal and visual aspects of a performance.

Form: The organization of the components of the song (intro, verse, chorus, interlude, tag, etc.); see construction.

Formants: A series of broad resonant-frequency bands that correspond to the natural resonant frequencies of the vocal tract.
Forte: Loud.
Fortissimo: Very loud.
Forward Motion: The sense of progress of the presentation—that is, the use of tempo, dynamics, volume, interpretive devices, and physical movement to create energy, musicality, and interest in a presentation.
Four-Part Chord: A chord that contains four notes, none of which share the same name.
Free Style: The style in which a song segment is presented without regard to a regular meter or rhythm; see ad lib and rubato.
Frequency: The number of periodic vibrations or cycles occurring per second in a musical tone; see hertz.
Fullness: The sense of space or size of a sound, not to be confused with volume.
Fundamental: The name for the harmonic of the lowest frequency of a harmonic series.
Gang Singing: Informal group singing.
Gestures: Physical movements intended to illustrate or amplify the theme of the song.
Glimmer: A party held after an everglow; see preglow and afterglow.
Glissando: Gliding from one pitch to another, also "gliss"; see portamento.
Glottal Attack/Release: The beginning or ending of voiced sound resulting from the sudden release of pressure beneath the vocal folds.
Glottis: The opening between the vocal folds.
Half Step: In Western music, the smallest interval between two notes.
Harmonic: (1) Tones of higher pitch that are present in a regular series in sound and whose relative intensity determines the timbre of the musical sound (see overtone and partial); (2) of, relating to, or characterized by musical harmony.
Harmonic Movement: The progression from chord to chord in music.
Harmonic Series: A theoretically infinite number of tones whose frequencies are small whole-number multiples of the frequency of a pure fundamental note.
Harmonization: Setting harmony parts to a melody.

Harmony: The simultaneous combination of tones into chords.

Harmony, Incorporated: Also Harmony, Inc., an organization formed to preserve and promote barbershop harmony for women; see Barbershop Harmony Society and Sweet Adelines International.

Head Register: See head voice.

Head Voice: A kind of vocal production that commonly occurs in the higher range; see head register.

Hertz (Hz): The number of cycles per second (cps) of a pitch.

Homophony/Homophonic: Music in which one voice part carries the melody and is supported by chord tones in the other voice parts, with all voice parts moving together in the same rhythm, on the same words; see polyphony/polyphonic.

Horizontal Tuning: The tuning method used by melody singers, closely approximating the equal temperament of the keyboard but adjusted at appropriate places to maintain the tonal center; see vertical tuning.

Implied Harmony: A succession of harmonies and chord progressions suggested by the song's melody.

Incomplete Chord: A chord in which one or more of the notes that define the chord are missing.

Inflection: A distinctive emphasis of volume or color for effect; pulsation.

Intensity: A focus of physical or vocal energy to convey an emotion or energy in a musical presentation.

International: (1) The largest geographical unit of the Barbershop Harmony Society, Sweet Adelines International, and Harmony, Incorporated; (2) the site of the main annual conventions and competitions of each organization.

Interpolation: The insertion of a short segment from another song into an arrangement.

Interpretation: The performer's musical and physical choices to convey the meaning, intent, and emotion of the song.

Interval: The distance between two notes.

Intonation: (1) The degree to which the tonal center in a song remains invariant; (2) the degree of maintenance of just intonation intervals between the harmony parts and the melody.

Intro: A composed musical introduction to an arrangement.

Just Intonation: A method of tuning that relies on intervals derived from the overtone series.

Key: (1) The scale on which a song is based; (2) the tonic pitch or tonic chord that defines the implied harmony of the melody.

Key Change: An arrangement device that causes the key of the arrangement to change.

Larynx: The narrow passageway in the throat containing the vocal folds.

Lead: (1) The second-highest part, generally, in a quartet; (2) the singer who sings the melody in a quartet.

Leading Tone: (1) A note that implies a movement to another tone a half-step higher or lower; (2) the unaltered seventh note of a major scale that leads melodically to the tonic; see major seventh.

Legato: Smooth progression from note to note in a musical line.

Lock: The sound associated with a justly in-tune chord; see just intonation.

Lock and Ring: The sound associated with the simultaneous pairing of lock and ring.

Loudness: The magnitude of the auditory sensation produced by sound waves; see volume.

Lyrical: Having an artistic or expressive quality.

Lyrics: The words of a song.

Major-Minor Seventh Chord: A chord that in root position is composed of a major third (four half steps) below two minor thirds (three half steps); see barbershop seventh.

Major Scale: A scale in Western music that contains the pattern of two whole steps, one half step, three whole steps, and one half step; see diatonic scale.

Major Seventh: (1) The unaltered seventh tone of a major scale; (2) the interval between the root and the seventh of a major scale.

Marcato: A strong sense of pulsation or accent.

Medley: A construction in which major portions of two or more songs are used in an arrangement.

Melody: The pattern of notes of a song.

Meter: The orderly pattern of beats and measures of a song.

Mezzo Forte: Moderately loud.

Mezzo Piano: Moderately soft.

Migration: The natural tendency to change vowel sound and timbre with changes of pitch or volume.

GLOSSARY

Mix: The combining and balancing of the head and chest registers, usually in the middle range.

Modification: The adjustment of the vocal tract to enhance vowel resonance.

Musicality: Artistic sensitivity to the meaning, emotion, and intent of a musical composition or arrangement.

Nonsinging Time: Those parts of a performance that occur when the ensemble is not singing.

Note: A pitch in a chord or musical scale that has been assigned a name in Western music.

Octave: The interval between one musical pitch and another with half or double its frequency.

Overtones: Harmonics of second order or higher; it is usual to refer to the first overtone as the second harmonic, the second overtone as the third harmonic, and so on.

Parallel Fifths: Movement of any two voice parts that maintains an interval of a perfect fifth between the parts.

Part: One of the voices in a quartet, see tenor, lead, baritone, and bass; see also voice part.

Partials: See overtones.

Patter: An arrangement device that juxtaposes a melodic line against harmony parts and uses shorter note durations and more frequent syllables.

Pause/Grand Pause: See fermata.

Peel-Off: An arrangement device that causes a sung unison to spread into a chord without break in the sound; see cascade.

Performance: A presentation of the song, as arranged, for the entertainment of an audience; see presentation.

Pharynx: The area of the throat above the larynx extending upward behind the mouth and nose.

Phrasing: In performance, the process of connecting successive tones in a melody to convey the intent, emotion, or meaning of the song.

Pianissimo: Very soft.

Pick-Up Quartet: An informal grouping of four singers.

Ping: The audible presence of high frequencies in a vocal tone.

Pitch: The number of cycles per second (or hertz) at which a sound vibrates.

Pitch Pipe: A device used to sound a pitch.

Polecat: A commonly known barbershop arrangement; see chestnut.

Polyphony/Polyphonic: Music that combines more than one melodic line; see homophony/homophonic.

Portamento: The process of sliding from one pitch to another; see glissando.

Post: (1) A note of long duration against which multiple successive harmony notes are sung, creating a progression of chords; (2) a held note in a tag.

Precision: Coordination of attacks, releases, vowels, diphthongs, volume changes, physical movement, and so on; see synchronization.

Preglow: A party held before a barbershop event.

Presentation: The way a musical performance is delivered; see performance.

Projective Modes: The three means—facial expression, vocal sound, and gesture/body language—that a singer uses to communicate the emotional message of a song.

Props: Portable inanimate articles used to enhance a presentation.

Pulse Beat: (1) The stress beat or metronomic pulse in a composition; (2) the rhythmic pulse on which the primary vowel sound should occur.

Punch Line: Occasion of major surprise, incongruity, or other comedic impact in a performance.

Push Beat: The accent of a syncopated pulse in a rhythmic meter.

PVI: Personal vocal instruction, a period of individualized vocal instruction.

Pythagorean comma: In Pythagorean tuning, the small interval between two enharmonically equivalent notes, such as B♭ and A♯, caused by the difference between the chromatic and diatonic half step in that tuning method. In tuning barbershop in just intonation, this discrepancy causes a slight lowering of key center when the harmony proceeds precisely in tune around the circle of fifths.

Railroad Tracks: The musical symbol indicating a pause in the music, the length of which is at the performer's discretion, indicated by double oblique lines; also "caesura."

Region: The major geographical subdivision of Sweet Adelines International; see area, district, and international.

Register: A range of tones whose vocal fold vibration is controlled by a particular set of muscles; see chest register and head register.
Release: The termination or cessation of sound.
Resonance: The amplification of vocal sound in the pharyngeal cavity or throat.
Resonator: A cavity that amplifies and reinforces the initial sound produced.
Rest: A suspension of the lyric, melody, or physical motion for a specified duration.
Rhythm: An organized pattern of regular beats in successive measures of a song.
Ring: The presence of audible overtones in a sound.
Riser Buddy: A person designated to help a visitor or new member gain familiarity with the culture of a chapter.
Root: The pitch to which all notes of a chord are related.
Root Position: A chord in which the root of the chord is the lowest tone.
Rubato: A moderate variation of tempo or duration of notes while maintaining a sense of meter; see ad lib and free style.
Scale: A succession of musical notes ordered by pitch.
Scissors: An arrangement device that features two or more parts moving in contrary motion.
Second Inversion: A chord in which the fifth of the chord is the lowest tone.
Sets: Large, fixed articles of staging intended to enhance a presentation.
Seventh: The seventh scale degree. When functioning as a harmony note, is usually lowered one half step; see flat seventh.
Sixth: The sixth scale degree of the diatonic scale; a dissonant note used for color in the barbershop style.
Song: The composer's melody, lyrics, rhythm, and implied harmony.
Staccato: The style of separate, detached execution of notes.
Stage Presence: The physical persona of the performer as it relates to comfort or command of the stage and the music being performed.
Strong Voicing: A chord in which the root or fifth of the chord is the lowest note and contains no divorced tones.
Subglottal Pressure: Breath pressure below the vocal folds; see glottal attack/release.

Sum Tone: A combination tone produced by the sum of the different frequencies of two or more pitches.

Sweet Adelines International: The largest all-female organization formed to preserve and promote barbershop harmony; see Barbershop Harmony Society and Harmony, Incorporated.

Swing Tune: (1) A song with a regular tempo that emphasizes weak beats and that lengthens the first of two successive eighth notes to the duration of the first two beats of an eighth-note triplet; (2) songs from the swing era in popular American music.

Swipe: An arrangement device in which one or more parts change pitch while the other parts maintain pitch, usually employing a single syllable.

Synchronization: The degree of coordination achieved in the execution of chord progressions and word sounds; see precision.

Syncopation: The placing of notes or accents in unexpected places in a musical line, interrupting the regular metrical flow of the beats.

Tag: A composed section at the end of an arrangement that restates the melodic or lyrical content of the song, corresponding loosely to a coda in Western music.

Tempered Scale: See equal temperament.

Tempo: The rate of speed of the beats of a song.

Tenor: (1) The highest harmony part in a quartet; (2) the singer who sings the highest harmony part in a quartet.

Tenuto: A slight lengthening of the duration of a note.

Tessitura: (1) The general "lie" of a vocal part, either "high or "low" in range; (2) the pitch range in which a singer is most comfortable.

Theme: (1) The essential element in the music; (2) the composer or arranger's basic intent for the song or arrangement.

Third: The third scale degree. When functioning as a harmony note, it should be sung less loudly than the root and fifth of the chord to minimize the dissonance of its harmonic series with that of the harmonic series of the root and fifth.

Third Inversion Chord: A chord in which the third note above the theoretical root is the lowest tone.

Timbre: The harmonic profile or sound quality of a sound source or instrument.

Timing: The sensitivity of the performer to action/reaction moments in the presentation and the effect on communication with the audience.

GLOSSARY

Tonal Center: The key note of the melodic phrase or series of phrases, used to define the beginning and ending of the chord progressions implied by the melody.

Tone Color: See timbre.

Tonic: The first scale step or key note of a scale.

Tonic Chord: Three or more notes sounded together, the root of which is the tonic, that correspond to the harmonic center of the melody and its implied harmony.

Tremolo: Excessive vibrato.

Tritone: (1) A musical interval of three whole tones; (2) the dissonant interval between the third and the flat seventh in a barbershop-seventh chord that resolves to the consonant interval of the major third in the next chord in the circle of fifths, inducing harmonic movement.

Tuning: The act of adjusting pitches to achieve a desired level of consonance in the resulting sound.

Unison: Two or more voices sounding the same pitch simultaneously.

Untempered: (1) Referring to just intonation; (2) as opposed to a tempered scale.

Uptune: A song that has a quick, regular meter as its primary rhythmic pace, usually with an emphasis on strong beats (beats 1 and 3 in 4/4 meter).

Vertical Tuning: The tuning employed by harmony singers to maximize the reinforcement of harmonics, thus contributing to the amount of lock and ring in the barbershop sound; see just intonation and horizontal tuning.

Vibrato: A regular, pulsating change in pitch.

VLQ: A "very large quartet"—originally between five and sixteen voices, now of indeterminate size—larger than a quartet but smaller than a chorus.

Vocal Cords: See vocal folds.

Vocal Folds: Two folds of membranous tissue that project in from the sides of the larynx, which when excited by an air stream, vibrate and create sound.

Voice Leading: The writing of voice parts so that the movement from note to note is as smooth and effortless as possible.

Voice Part: See part.

Voicing: The distribution of voice parts relative to one another; see closed voicing and strong voicing.

Volume: In music, the relative loudness of the ensemble sound; see loudness.

Whole Step: The interval of two half steps.

Woodshedding: Harmonizing to a melody without a written arrangement; harmonizing "by ear"; see AHSOW.

APPENDIX A

Resources

Fortunately for persons looking for information and/or resources to aid them in singing barbershop, the major resources available are all assembled under the auspices of the three North American barbershop organizations. One only has to visit the website of each group to discover information in many categories: barbershop history, names and locations of choruses and quartets, music for sale, educational books and articles, DVDs of barbershop chorus and quartet performances, news about events past and future, information on competitions, and much, much more. There are also helpful staff members at the headquarters of each group, who are most eager to assist people in locating the information they need.[1]

    Barbershop Harmony Society (men)
    Sweet Adelines International (women)
    Harmony, Inc. (women)

In addition to these three websites, another excellent source for locating recordings of barbershop performances is YouTube. Once on the YouTube site, a search for "barbershop" brings up a large selection of recordings of barbershop ensembles in performances, both formal and informal. An extensive list of barbershop recordings can be found on the National Association of Teachers of Singing website in the So You Want to Sing Barbershop Online Resources section.

For personal contact with barbershoppers in your local area, refer to appendix B: "How to Locate a Barbershop Chapter or Chorus."

NOTE

1. For a link to the websites mentioned in this appendix, please visit this book's companion web page on the National Association of Teachers of Singing website.

APPENDIX B

How to Locate a Barbershop Chapter or Chorus

Let us say that you have read this book and decided that barbershop singing sounds like something you might enjoy. Now you would like to locate a chapter/chorus near where you live and visit the group to see if barbershop singing really is for you. How do you go about locating such a group?

The easiest way to locate a chapter is to visit the websites of the main barbershop organizations. They are all eager to help you find a chapter. Men should visit the site of the Barbershop Harmony Society.[1] On the home page there is a button to select: "Find a Group Today." Selecting this button takes you to the page for finding a chapter in the United States and Canada. You can search "by proximity" to find a chapter twenty-five to two hundred miles from you. For example, if you search for a chapter within fifty miles of Ripley, Tennessee, you will be directed to the RSVP Chapter in Germantown, which is near Memphis. If you search for a chapter in Memphis, you will be directed to two chapters: RSVP and the Memphis Men of Harmony. You can investigate the individual websites of each chapter to learn about the group and find out when and where they gather to rehearse. You can search "by name" if you know the name of a chapter or even part of a name. If you happen to have heard the name "Westminster" and type that in, you will be directed to the Westminster Chorus in Anaheim, California. Last but not least, you can search "by district." A list of the districts is given, and you can click on each district name to discover a list of the chapters that make up that district. With a little more sleuthing within the list, you can find a chapter that may suit your needs. Almost all the chapters have individual websites, and they typically offer e-mail addresses for contact persons who can answer any questions you may have.

The women also make it easy to locate a chapter. You have two choices of organizations, Sweet Adelines International or Harmony, Inc., both of which also have websites.[2] On the Sweet Adelines home page, you can select the button "Find a Chorus." You are then directed to a page that allows you several search options. First, you can search "by zip code." If you type in the zip code 49686 and a radius of fifty miles, you will be directed to the Grand Traverse Show Chapter in Traverse City, Michigan. You can search "by city and state." If you type in "Houston, Texas," and a radius of twenty-five miles, you will be directed to the Houston Horizon Chapter. You can search "by country." If you type in "Sweden," you will be directed to a list of sixteen choruses. In each case, a map is given, showing the geographical location of the chapter or chapters that you are seeking. Again, most of the groups have individual websites where you can find information and the names of contact persons. Likewise, on the Harmony, Inc., home page, you can select a link that says "Chapters" and then "Locate a Chapter." A map appears that shows the United States and Canada and the seven areas of Harmony, Inc. If you live in Virginia, you can easily see that this state is in "Area 3." When you select "Area 3," you are directed to a list of twelve chapters, and in perusing the list, you can locate the Bella Nova Chorus in Herndon, Virginia.

Of course, due to the fluid nature of modern technology, it is possible that by the time you visit these websites to look for a chapter, some of the instruction buttons may have changed. But the principle will remain the same. If you persevere, you should be able to discover the plan and find a barbershop chorus somewhere in your vicinity. It is true that there may not be a barbershop chorus right in your town, unless you live in a major city, but many, many barbershoppers are happy to drive some distance to pursue this exciting kind of singing. Sometimes carpooling is half the fun! At any rate, the organizations make it easy for you to find the nearest opportunity to engage in four-part a cappella harmony, barbershop style.

NOTES

1. For a link to this and other websites mentioned in this appendix, please visit this book's companion web page on the National Association of Teachers of Singing website.

2. See note 1, above.

APPENDIX C

International Quartet and Chorus Champions

BARBERSHOP HARMONY SOCIETY

2016—Nashville, TN. Forefront; Ambassadors of Harmony Chorus (St. Charles, MO). Senior Quartet (SQ)—High Priority. College Quartet (CQ)—Pratt Street Power

2015—Pittsburgh, PA. Instant Classic; Westminster Chorus (Westminster, CA). SQ—Saturday Evening Post. CQ—Trocadero

2014—Las Vegas, NV. Musical Island Boys; Vocal Majority Chorus (Dallas, TX). SQ—Faces 4 Radio. CQ—The Academy

2013—Toronto, ON. Masterpiece; Toronto Northern Lights Chorus (Toronto, ON). SQ—Border Patrol. CQ—The Newfangled Four

2012—Portland, OR. Ringmasters; Ambassadors of Harmony Chorus (St. Charles, MO). SQ—Rusty Pipes. CQ—Lemon Squeezy

2011—Kansas City, MO. Old School; Masters of Harmony Chorus (Santa Fe Springs, CA). SQ—Over Easy. CQ—Prestige

2010—Philadelphia, PA. Storm Front; Westminster Chorus (Westminster, CA). SQ—Resisting-A-Rest. CQ—Swedish Match

2009—Anaheim, CA. Crossroads; Ambassadors of Harmony Chorus (St. Charles, MO). SQ—Audacity. CQ—The Vagrants

2008—Nashville, TN. OC Times; Masters of Harmony Chorus (Santa Fe Springs, CA). SQ—Eureka! CQ—Ringmasters

2007—Denver, CO. Max Q; Westminster Chorus (Westminster, CA). SQ—Friendly Advice. CQ—Road Trip

2006—Indianapolis, IN. Vocal Spectrum; Vocal Majority Chorus (Dallas, TX). SQ—Antique Gold. CQ—Musical Island Boys

2005—Salt Lake City, UT. Realtime; Masters of Harmony Chorus (Santa Fe Springs, CA). SQ—Texoma Sound. CQ—Men in Black

2004—Louisville, KY. Gotcha!; Ambassadors of Harmony Chorus (St. Charles, MO). SQ—Downstate Express. CQ—Vocal Spectrum

2003—Montreal, QB. Power Play; Vocal Majority Chorus (Dallas, TX). SQ—The Barons. CQ—HEAT

2002—Portland, OR. Four Voices; Masters of Harmony Chorus (Santa Fe Springs, CA). SQ—Chicago Shuffle. CQ—Catfish Bend

2001—Nashville, TN. Michigan Jake; New Tradition Chorus (Northbrook, IL). SQ—Harmony. CQ—Reprise

2000—Kansas City, MO. PLATINUM; Vocal Majority Chorus (Dallas, TX). SQ—OVER TIME. CQ—Millennium

1999—Anaheim, CA. FRED; Masters of Harmony Chorus (Santa Fe Springs, CA). SQ—Tri-County Reclamation Project. CQ—Station 59

1998—Atlanta, GA. Revival; Alexandria Harmonizers (Alexandria, VA). SQ—Jurassic Larks. CQ—Prime Cut

1997—Indianapolis, IN. Yesteryear; Vocal Majority Chorus (Dallas, TX). SQ—Saturday's Heroes. CQ—Freefall

1996—Salt Lake City, UT. Nightlife; Masters of Harmony Chorus (Santa Fe Springs, CA). SQ—Fatherly Advice. CQ—Four Voices

1995—Miami Beach, FL. Marquis; Alexandria Harmonizers (Alexandria, VA). SQ—Reminisce. CQ—Stop the Presses

1994—Pittsburgh, PA. Joker's Wild; Vocal Majority Chorus (Dallas, TX). SQ—The New and Improved Industrial Strength Mini-Chorus. CQ—The Real Deal

1993—Calgary, AB, Canada. The Gas House Gang; Masters of Harmony Chorus (Foothills Cities, CA). SQ—Rockies 4. CQ—Heritage Station

1992—New Orleans, LA. Keepsake; Southern Gateway Chorus (Western Hills, OH). SQ—One More Time. CQ—Waterstreet Junction

1991—Louisville, KY. The Ritz; Vocal Majority Chorus (Dallas, TX). SQ—Old Kids on the Block

1990—San Francisco, CA. Acoustix; Masters of Harmony Chorus (Foothills Cities, CA). SQ—Grandma's Beans

1989—Kansas City, MO. Second Edition; Alexandria Harmonizers (Alexandria, VA). SQ—Bayou City Music Committee

1988—San Antonio, TX. Chiefs of Staff; Vocal Majority Chorus (Dallas, TX). SQ—Silvertones

1987—Hartford, CT. Interstate Rivals; West Towns Chorus (Lombard, IL). SQ—Close Harmony Tradition

1986—Salt Lake City, UT. Rural Route 4; Alexandria Harmonizers (Alexandria, VA). SQ—George Baggish Memorial Quartet

1985—Minneapolis, MN. The New Tradition; Vocal Majority Chorus (Dallas, TX)

1984—St. Louis, MO. The Rapscallions; Thoroughbreds Chorus (Louisville, KY)

1983—Seattle, WA. Side Street Ramblers; Phoenicians Chorus (Phoenix, AZ)

1982—Pittsburgh, PA. Classic Collection; Vocal Majority Chorus (Dallas, TX)

1981—Detroit, MI. Chicago News; Thoroughbreds Chorus (Louisville, KY)

1980—Salt Lake City, UT. Boston Common; Dukes of Harmony Chorus (Scarborough, ON)

1979—Minneapolis, MN. Grandma's Boys; Vocal Majority Chorus (Dallas, TX)

1978—Cincinnati, OH. Bluegrass Student Union; Thoroughbreds Chorus (Louisville, KY)

1977—Philadelphia, PA. Most Happy Fellows; Dukes of Harmony Chorus (Scarborough, ON)

1976—San Francisco, CA. The Innsiders; Phoenicians Chorus (Phoenix, AZ)

1975—Indianapolis, IN. Happiness Emporium; Vocal Majority Chorus (Dallas, TX)

1974—Kansas City, MO. The Regents; Vocal Majority Chorus (Dallas, TX)

1973—Portland, OR. Dealer's Choice; Southern Gateway Chorus (Western Hills, OH)
1972—Atlanta, GA. Golden Staters; Phoenicians Chorus (Phoenix, AZ)
1971—New Orleans, LA. Gentlemen's Agreement; Chorus of the Chesapeake (Dundalk, MD)
1970—Atlantic City, NJ. Oriole Four; Dapper Dans of Harmony Chorus (Livingston, NJ)
1969—St. Louis, MO. Mark IV; Thoroughbreds Chorus (Louisville, KY)
1968—Cincinnati, OH. Western Continentals; Pekin Chorus (Pekin, IL)
1967—Los Angeles, NV. Four Statesmen; Dapper Dans of Harmony Chorus (Livingston, NJ)
1966—Chicago, IL. Auto Towners; Thoroughbreds Chorus (Louisville, KY)
1965—Boston, MA. Four Renegades; Miamians Chorus (Miami, FL)
1964—San Antonio, TX. Sidewinders; Border Chorders Chorus (El Paso, TX)
1963—Toronto, ON. Town and Country Four; Pekin Chorus (Pekin, IL)
1962—Kansas City, MO. Gala Lads; Thoroughbreds Chorus (Louisville, KY)
1961—Philadelphia, PA. Suntones; Chorus of the Chesapeake (Dundalk, MD)
1960—Dallas, TX. Evans Quartet; Chordsmen Chorus (San Antonio, TX)
1959—Chicago, IL. Four Pitchikers; Pekin Chorus (Pekin, IL)
1958—Columbus, OH. Gaynotes; Dixie Cotton Bowl Chorus (Memphis, TN)
1957—Los Angeles, CA. Lads of Enchantment; Californians Chorus (Berkeley, CA)
1956—Minneapolis, MN. Confederates; Ambassadors of Harmony Chorus (Michigan City, IN)
1955—Miami Beach, FL. Four Hearsemen; Janesville Chorus (Janesville, WI)

1954—Washington, DC. Orphans; Singing Capital Chorus (Washington, DC)
1953—Detroit, MI. Vikings; Great Lakes Chorus (Grand Rapids, MI)
1952—Kansas City, MO. Four Teens
1951—Toledo, OH. Schmitt Brothers
1950—Omaha, NE. Buffalo Bills
1949—Buffalo, NY. Mid-States Four
1948—Oklahoma City, OK. Pittsburghers
1947—Milwaukee, WI. Doctors of Harmony
1946—Cleveland, OH. Garden State Quartet
1945—Detroit, MI. Misfits
1944—Detroit, MI. Harmony Halls
1943—Chicago, IL. Four Harmonizers
1942—Grand Rapids, MI. Elastic Four
1941—St. Louis, MO. Chordbusters
1940—New York, NY. Flat Foot Four
1939—Tulsa, OK. Bartlesville Barflies

SWEET ADELINES INTERNATIONAL

2016—Las Vegas, NV. Frenzy (Canada); Rönninge Show Chorus (Rönninge, Sweden). Division A Chorus (A)—Carpe Diem. Division AA Chorus (AA)—Pearls of the Sound. Auckland, New Zealand. Rising Star Quartet (RSQ)—The Ladies
2015—Las Vegas, NV. Speed of Sound (NC); Scottsdale Chorus (Scottsdale, AZ). A—Carolina Harmony. AA—River Blenders. Scottsdale, AZ. RSQ—C'est la Vie
2014—Baltimore, MD. Bling! (FL); Melodeers Chorus (Northbrook, IL). A—Springfield Metro. AA—City of Gardens. Lowell, MA. RSQ—ClassRing
2013—Honolulu, HI. Lovenotes (CA); Rönninge Show Chorus (Rönninge, Sweden). A—Pearls of the Sound. AA—Rhythm of the Rockies
2012—Denver, CO. Touché (FL); North Metro Chorus (Toronto, ON). A—Carolina Harmony. AA—West Coast Harmony. RSQ—GQ

2011—Houston, TX. Martini (Canada); Melodeers Chorus (Northbrook, IL). A—Alba Show. AA—Metro Nashville. RSQ—The Fource

2010—Seattle, WA. Maxx Factor (MD); Scottsdale Chorus (Scottsdale, AZ). A—Queen City Sound. AA—Harbor City Music Company. RSQ—Royal Blush

2009—Nashville, TN. Zing! (KS); Rich-Tone Chorus (Richardson, TX). A—Millennium Magic. AA—Scioto Valley. RSQ—Vogue

2008—Honolulu, HI. Moxie Ladies (OH); Melodeers Chorus (Northbrook, IL). A—Stockholm City Voices. AA—Metro Nashville. San Antonio, TX. RSQ—Whole Lotta Harmony

2007—Calgary, AB. Four Bettys (IL); Harborlites Chorus (Anaheim, CA). San Antonio, TX. A—Alba Show. AA—Waikato Rivertones. RSQ—Luminous

2006—Las Vegas, NV. Salt (Sweden); Rich-Tone Chorus (Richardson, TX). San Antonio, TX. A—Metro Nashville. AA—Harbor City Music Company. RSQ—Footnotes

2005—Detroit, MI. Spotlight (MI & OH); Scottsdale Chorus (Scottsdale, AZ). Greenville, SC. A—Women of Note. AA—Scioto Valley. RSQ—UnderAge

2004—Indianapolis, IN. The Buzz (NJ); Harborlites Chorus (Anaheim, CA). Greenville, SC. A—Queen City. AA—Columbus. RSQ—Tone Appétit

2003—Phoenix, AZ. Brava! (Canada); Melodeers Chorus (Northbrook, IL). Greenville, SC. A—Millennium Magic. AA—Valley Forge. RSQ—BarbieShop

2002—Nashville, TN. Swinglish Mix (KY); North Metro Chorus (Toronto, ON). Greenville, SC. A—Prairie Echoes. AA—Royal River. RSQ—Voice Activated

2001—Portland, OR. Fanatix (CA); San Diego Chorus (San Diego, CA). San Antonio, TX. A—Pearls of the Sound. AA—Jacksonville Harmony. RSQ—Backchat

2000—Orlando, FL. A Cappella Gold (CA); Melodeers Chorus (Northbrook, IL). San Antonio, TX. A—Prairie Echoes. AA—Royal River. RSQ—Sandstone

1999—Atlanta, GA. Signature Sound (MD); North Metro Chorus (Toronto, ON). San Antonio, TX. RSQ—Dazzling Diamonds

1998—Nashville, TN. Rumors (TX); Rich-Tone Chorus (Richardson, TX)

1997—Salt Lake City, UT. Classic Edition (KS); Melodeers Chorus (Northbrook, IL)

1996—Fort Lauderdale, FL. 4-Star Collection (MN); North Metro Chorus (Toronto, ON)

1995—New Orleans, LA. Weekend Edition (MO); Rich-Tone Chorus (Richardson, TX)

1994—Reno, NV. Chicago Fire (IL); Melodeers Chorus (Northbrook, IL)

1993—Indianapolis, IN. Showtime (FL); Toast of Tampa Chorus (Tampa, FL)

1992—Baltimore, MD. City Lights (NJ); Rich-Tone Chorus (Richardson, TX)

1991—San Antonio, TX. Swing Street (MI & OH); Gem City Chorus (Dayton, OH)

1990—Salt Lake City, UT. Panache (CA); Ramapo Valley Chorus (Upper Saddle River, NJ)

1989—Miami Beach, FL. Growing Girls (Sweden); Scottsdale Chorus (Scottsdale, AZ)

1988—Houston, TX. Savvy (CA); Vienna-Falls Chorus (Fairfax, VA)

1987—Honolulu, HI. Ginger 'n' Jazz (OK); High Country Chorus (Denver, CO)

1986—Philadelphia, PA. Ambiance (IL & MO); Ramapo Valley Chorus (Upper Saddle River, NJ)

1985—Kansas City, MO. Jubilation (IL); Gem City Chorus (Dayton, OH)

1984—Las Vegas, NV. 4-for-the-Show (CA); Scottsdale Chorus (Scottsdale, AZ)

1983—Detroit, MI. Melo-Edge (IL); Valley Forge Chorus (Valley Forge, PA)

1982—Minneapolis, MN. Music Gallery (MN); Gem City Chorus (Dayton, OH)

1981—Phoenix, AZ. All-Star Jubilee (CO); Seven Hills Chorus (Cincinnati, OH)

1980—Atlanta, GA. Penna-Fores (PA); High Country Chorus (Denver, CO)

1979—St. Louis, MO. Hallmarks (MO); Ramapo Valley Chorus (Upper Saddle River, NJ)
1978—Los Angeles, CA. Tetrachords (MO); Island Hills Chorus (Huntington, NY)
1977—London, England. Shondells (KS); Gem City Chorus (Dayton, OH)
1976—Cincinnati, OH. High Society (CA); Mission Valley Chorus (Santa Clara, CA)
1975—Seattle, WA. Front Office 4 (MI); San Diego Chorus (San Diego, CA)
1974—Milwaukee, WI. Sounds of Music (OH); Gem City Chorus (Dayton, OH)
1973—Washington, DC. Tiffanys (IL); Racine Chorus (Racine, WI)
1972—Salt Lake City, UT. Fourth Edition (OH)
1971—Kansas City, MO. Bron's Tones (AL)
1970—Boston, MA. Rarities (WI)
1969—Honolulu, HI. Metropolitans (CA)
1968—Oklahoma City, OK. Galatones (IA)
1967—New York, NY. Hurricane Honeys (FL)
1966—Houston, TX. Piper-Ettes (OH)
1965—Denver, CO. Shalimars (CA)
1964—Minneapolis, MN. Note-Cracker Sweets (MN)
1963—Berkeley, CA. Heathertones (OH)
1962—Toronto, ON. Sea-Adelines (WA)
1961—Colorado Springs, CO. Lyrics (IL)
1960—Detroit, MI. Gibson Girls (PA)
1959—Tucson, AZ. Yankee Misses (MI)
1958—Peoria, IL. Sweet and Lows (IL)
1957—Miami Beach, FL. Cracker Jills (MI)
1956—Wichita, KS. Junior Misses (IL)
1955—Grand Rapids, MI. Nota-Belles (IL)
1954—Buffalo, NY. Mississippi Misses (IA)
1953—Milwaukee, WI. Big Four (IL)
1952—St. Petersburg, FL. Pitch Pipers (IL)
1951—Santa Monica, CA. Quarternotes (WI)
1950—Chicago, IL. Harmony Belles (CA)
1949—St. Louis, MO. Tune Twisters (IL)

1948—Topeka, KS. Johnson Sisters (IL)
1947—Tulsa, OK. Decaturettes (IL)

HARMONY, INC.

2016—Taken 4 Granite (Area 2); A Cappella Showcase Chorus (Milton, ON)
2015—Livewire (Area 3); Village Vocal Chords Chorus (Chicago, IL)
2014—Moonstruck (Area 2); New England Voices in Harmony Chorus (Nashua, NH)
2013—Spot On (Area 4); Village Vocal Chords Chorus (Chicago, IL)
2012—Epic (Area 2); A Cappella Showcase Chorus (Milton, ON)
2011—Foreign Exchange (Area 2); Village Vocal Chords Chorus (Chicago, IL)
2010—Ringtones! (Area 2); Northern Blend, Inc., Chorus (Watertown, NY)
2009—Showcase (Area 2); Village Vocal Chords Chorus (Chicago, IL)
2008—U4X (Areas 3 & 4); A Cappella Showcase Chorus (Milton, ON, Canada)
2007—Mystique (Area 3); Village Vocal Chords Chorus (Chicago, IL)
2006—Boston Accent (Area 2); Derby City Chorus (Louisville, KY)
2005—Exhilaration (Area 2); Village Vocal Chords Chorus (Chicago, IL)
2004—Synchronicity (Area 2); Derby City Chorus (Louisville, KY)
2003—Hot Topic (Area 4); Village Vocal Chords Chorus (Chicago, IL)
2002—Voices (Area 4); Derby City Chorus (Louisville, KY)
2001—Upstate Rhythm (Area 3); Village Vocal Chords Chorus (Chicago, IL)
2000—After Hours (Area 2); Derby City Chorus (Louisville, KY)
1999—Change of Heart (Area 4); Village Vocal Chords Chorus (Chicago, IL)
1998—Blue Champagne (Area 2); Derby City Chorus (Louisville, KY)
1997—Images (Area 3); Village Vocal Chords Chorus (Chicago, IL)

1996—For Heaven's Sake (Area 3); Capital Chordettes, Inc., Chorus (Ottawa, ON)
1995—Limited Edition (Area 2); Village Vocal Chords Chorus (Chicago, IL)
1994—Soundwave (Area 3); Pride of Niagara Chorus (Regional Municipality of Niagara, ON)
1993—Spectrum (Area 1); Village Vocal Chords Chorus (Chicago, IL)
1992—Sequel (Area 4); Champlain Echoes, Inc. Chorus (Burlington, VT)
1991—Metro Music Machine (Area 1); Village Vocal Chords Chorus (Chicago, IL)
1990—First Class (Area 4); Champlain Echoes, Inc. Chorus (Burlington, VT)
1989—Heart's Delight (Area 2); Village Vocal Chords Chorus (Chicago, IL)
1988—Talk of the Town (Area 2); Capital Chordettes, Inc., Chorus (Ottawa, ON)
1987—Kaleidoscope (Area 4); Village Vocal Chords Chorus (Chicago, IL)
1986—Four in Accord (Area 3); Champlain Echoes, Inc., Chorus (Burlington, VT)
1985—Cameo Performance (Area 4); Village Vocal Chords Chorus (Chicago, IL)
1984—Black Magic (Area 5); Capital Chordettes, Inc., Chorus (Ottawa, ON)
1983—Joy (Area 2); Village Vocal Chords Chorus (Chicago, IL)
1982—Chicago Chord Company (Area 4); Harmony First Chorus (Springfield, IL)
1981—Crystal Collection (Area 4); Village Vocal Chords Chorus (Chicago, IL)
1980—Keepsake (Area 3); Harmony First Chorus (Springfield, IL)
1979—The Spirit of Harmony (Area 3); Village Vocal Chords Chorus (Chicago, IL)
1978—A Good Arrangement (Area 4); The Over Tones Chorus (Guelph, ON)
1977—The Villagers (Area 4); The Harmonettes Chorus (North Attleboro, MA)

1976—Reflections (Area 4); Village Vocal Chords Chorus (Chicago, IL)
1975—Sound Pipers (Area 4); Quad-City Multi-Chords Chorus (Moline, IL)
1974—Esprit de Corps (Area 4); Northern-Aires Chorus (Rosemere, QB)
1973—Moline Tradition (Area 4); Valley Bells of Harmony Chorus (Elgin, IL)
1972—Chatelaines (Area 2); Multi-Chords Chorus (Moline, IL)
1971—On Chords (Area 4); The Harmonettes Chorus (North Attleboro, MA)
1970—Chord Teasers (Area 4); The Harmonettes Chorus (North Attleboro, MA)
1969—Pinkertones (Area 2); The Harmonettes Chorus (North Attleboro, MA)
1968—Quad-Ra-Tones (Area 4); Valley Bells of Harmony Chorus (Elgin, IL)
1967—Debonaires (Area 2); The Harmonettes Chorus (North Attleboro, MA)
1966—Sophisti-Kords (Area 4); Valley Bells of Harmony Chorus (Elgin, IL)
1965—Keynotes (Area 2)
1964—Scale Blazers (Area 4)
1963—Harmony Honeys (Area 2)
1962—Chord Jills (Area 2)
1961—Key Chords (Area 4)
1960—Pitch Pipe Pals (Area 2)

APPENDIX D

Choral Warm-ups—the Perfect Fifth— the Magic Interval
Val Hicks

The information below was created by Dr. Val Hicks, longtime barbershopper, music educator, composer, arranger, contest judge, coach, and clinician. We thank the Barbershop Harmony Society, to which the rights to Val's work were assigned upon his death, for allowing us to include this material.

The musical interval known as the perfect 5th [P5] is probably the most special interval of all those we sing. (An example would be C up to G.) Intervals when sounded simultaneously become harmonic and when sounded successively become melodic.

    Just as the number 2 gives birth to the octave, the number 3 creates harmony. When the length of a vibrating guitar string is doubled, the pitch drops one octave or when it is halved the pitch is heard an octave higher. With the same arithmetical operations using the number 3, the 5th is now brought into being. Two-ness only creates octaves: no harmony. Three-ness brings about the world of harmony: C to G to D to A to E to B to F-sharp, etc., or going downward C to F to B-flat to E-flat to A-flat, etc. You take all those pitches, gather them, organize them, and you have harmony. With the enharmonics (F-sharp = G-flat, C-sharp = D-flat, etc.) you have keys and scales, the gateway to songs, serenades and symphonies—and tags!

Many of our chords (in fact, most) contain, somewhere within the chord, a P5, so learning to sing that interval well in tune is vital. The two tones of the P5 can be between any two voices of the chord. When a P5 is in tune, it will feel and sound pure, unhampered by the commonplace or the mediocre. It has the spirit of excellence, unfettered by the tempered scale. It might even have a holiness about it. No matter how P5s affect you, utilize them. Use them as dear friends, for indeed, they are that.

Here are 20 exercises. You're not restricted to the key of C. In fact, change keys. Use different vowels, words, and/or syllables. Utilize solfege, scale numbers, and pitch names. Make these exercises fun. Don't get too serious. You will soon notice a change for the better in your intonation, both the vertical (chords) and the horizontal (parts).

CHORAL WARM-UPS—THE PERFECT FIFTH

Choral Warm-ups - The Perfect 5th - The Magic Interval - by Val Hicks

#1 *Gradually decrease the size of the half-steps until you achieve micro-tones.*

Tenors
Leads
Oo _____ Oo _____

Baritones
Basses

#2 *Sharp the 2nd degree and the 6th dregree ever so slightly*

Oo _____ Oo _____

#3   **#4**

#5

Too too   too, too too too ___ too   too _____

Copyright 1997 by Val Hicks. All rights reserved.

APPENDIX D

page 2

CHORAL WARM-UPS—THE PERFECT FIFTH 169

page 3

APPENDIX D

page 4

#16

#17

CHORAL WARM-UPS—THE PERFECT FIFTH 171

APPENDIX E

Ten Steps to a Better Singing and Performing Chorus
Greg Lyne

The following concepts were gleaned from a master class taught by Dr. Greg Lyne. These ten simple steps were the foundation on which he and his teams created two barbershop international champion choruses and have proven to be of help to ensembles of any size, skill level, or philosophy.

1. **Singer's posture.** Always sing with one foot slightly in front of the other, weight comfortably forward, chest comfortably up in a proud position, shoulders resting comfortably down and a little back, head in line with the body. Stand tall. Controlled relaxation is the goal, an attitude of readiness for anything. Everything in perfect equipoise!
2. **Active face.** Always sing with an involved face. Lift the cheek muscles a little, raise and lift the upper lip a little, energize the eyes a lot, get involved facially. No tortured looks, just energize the facial muscles.
3. **Vowels that look right.** Make an "oh" vowel look like an "oh" an "oo" like an "oo," and so on. Keep all the vowels vertical—not horizontal. Notice that a slight animation of the upper lip (a "lift" off the teeth) can contribute to increased resonation.

4. **Inline singing.** Make all the vowels sound similar. That is, no single vowel should "pop" out at the listener. They should all have a similar character. While an "ah" is certainly distinct from an "oh" or an "ee," it should not be vastly different in the way it's placed vocally or in its inherent resonant characteristics. This is achieved by consistent vocal production, consistent placement, and a consistent approach to the musical line. At its best, there should be a continual, uninterrupted resonance (ring) throughout the entire vocal line, through the full range of word sounds and pitches.
5. **Focused singing.** The sound is simply focused into a resonant point, about where the point of the unicorn's horn would be. Start the chorus with their hands held wide, shoulder high, and have them sing a unison pitch while slowly bringing the palms together in front of them. Have them listen to the "focusing" of the sound. This is related to number 4, above. They will feel the tone placed behind the eyes or a little higher. The tongue position is critical. The tongue should be relaxed, with the tip touching the lower gum ridge and the middle—or blade—raised to a comfortable, forward position. This should be carefully taught and carefully monitored. Excess tongue tension is counterproductive.
6. **Know the characteristics of your part.** There are many ways to relate the different roles of each part to the unified whole. I like the car analogy: The chorus is a finely tuned, extremely expensive racing machine (say, a Lamborghini). The basses are the engine: smooth, velvet, powerful, unrelenting in their supply of effortless power. The baris are the transmission: shifting from gear to gear in a smooth, effortless motion. The leads are, of course, the drivers. They are in control of both the speed and direction of this well-constructed machine. And the tenors are, well, how about the paint job? Brilliant yellow, fire-engine red?

    Of course, any descriptive approach to part characteristics (foundation from the basses, dignity from the baris, personality from the leads, shimmer or sparkle from the tenors) works equally well.
7. **Bring the whole singer.** Bring all that you have to offer to every experience in life, including the rehearsal. Be in the moment, be attentive, be alert, be energetic, contribute to the whole. "Be all that you can be."

8. **Expect to grow.** Expect every rehearsal to bring personal and corporate growth. Come with the expectation of learning. Come expecting the musical leadership to have something to teach you. Treat time spent not gaining new knowledge as time wasted. Mean to improve.
9. **"I'm talking to you!"** The director is talking to you! Not to the person behind you, not to the person on either side, not to the person in front, but to you. Every comment is meant for you. Be prepared to change instantly when the musical leader asks for a change. Don't think he or she means someone else. The director means you! Do it now! Only you can change the way the chorus performs.
10. **Look, act, be successful!** When you're a little down, your back or feet hurt, or you wish you were somewhere else, try acting the way you'd like to feel. Stand up straight, smile, elevate your chest, look someone in the eye. If you look successful and act successful, success will follow. Take charge of your experience and make it be something wonderful!

APPENDIX F

How to Learn a Song
*Paula Davis, Carolyn Sexton, and
Jay Giallombardo*

Barbershoppers don't hold the music when they sing in public. They memorize all the songs in the chorus or quartet repertoire, complete with choreography, musical interpretation, and the emotional content of the music and its lyrics. This can be intimidating to singers who come to barbershop from other choral traditions. The first time a visitor to a barbershop chorus rehearsal hears and sees a barbershop chorus in full flight, in "performance mode," the reaction is often, "Wow! I can never learn to do that!" But fear not. Like most things that take effort to master, it's a step-by-step process. The music is passed out, learning tracks are made available, section rehearsals are held, "early bird" choreography sessions are scheduled, individual help is given if needed—all enabling the chorister, who may not even really "read" music in the traditional sense of that term, to achieve an ease in performance that allows the musical intent of the composer and arranger to come through.

That said, it's helpful to have a plan when learning new songs. There are several methods of teaching and learning music used by barbershop organizations. Two of these methods are presented here. While the approaches are different, we feel both are valuable. Read them, apply their methodologies, and enjoy learning more rapidly and more durably, leading to the ultimate goal—sharing transcendent performances with your adoring public.

TWELVE-STEP PROGRAM TO LEARN MUSIC WITH LEARNING TRACKS

Developed in 1986 by Carolyn Sexton

Sweet Adelines International Development and Implementation of an Effective Rookie Program

Paula Davis

This is a twelve-step program to assist you in learning your music more successfully. It is only one system—over time, you may develop your own system that works best for you.

The success of this program is contingent upon the effective *listening skills* of the learner so much more than upon the musical background or ability to read music. Give it time! With each song, the process will become quicker.

Any of the twelve steps may be repeated before continuing on to the next step. But remember . . . *each* step is important to the overall successful results of learning *all* the right notes, words, and timing of the new song.

Do not eliminate any of the steps, even though they may appear to be insignificant to you. When you have passed your first song successfully, you'll be glad!

Step #1 *Listen* to the music while you close your eyes. (This will familiarize you with the general feel and flavor of the song.)

Step #2 *Watch* the *notes* on your music while you listen. Don't sing yet!

Step #3 Again, *watch* the *notes* while you listen. Don't sing yet!

Step #4 Watch the words on your music while you listen. Please— no singing yet!

Step #5 On a separate piece of paper, *write* down all the lyrics (you can refer to the music if needed). Now, watch your paper to check all you've written while you *listen* once again. Nope—no singing yet!

Step #6   *Watch* the *notes* again while you *listen*.

Step #7   *Watch* the *words* again while you *listen*.

Step #8   Try to write the words down again on another piece of paper without looking at the music. If you have trouble, listen to the track again while you watch the words. Then return to writing it again without looking.

Step #9   *Hurray!* Finally, you can add your voice! Now watch the notes on your music while you *hum* along. Hum—singing is next!

Step #10   *Watch* the words on your music while you sing along. Can you believe it—you're singing! However, if you have any difficulty, *circle* the spot on your music as you go through. Then go back and *listen* to those parts again.

Step #11   Record yourself singing your part all the way through *without* looking at your music.

Step #12   *Watch* your music and *listen* to your own recording to see if you are correct. You'll probably be outstanding! But if you have any doubt, go back and check your part again on the master recording.

Concentrate on listening to the parts you circled earlier to be sure you have made the corrections.

Congratulations!

With a little bit of luck plus all your great work, *you* are now the proud singer ready to qualify!

LEARNING A SONG

Jay Giallombardo

While there are many ways to learn music, some methods are more effective than others. When it comes to part singing, how you go about learning an arrangement will certainly affect the quality of your performance.

In a cappella singing, barbershop specifically, tuning—that is, the locking and ringing of chords—is a hallmark of the style. How you go about learning a piece will have a considerable impact on how well you stay in key and how well you tune chords.

There are three things that affect tuning: (1) pitch, (2) volume/balance, and (3) color. Of course, learning pitches is actually the easy part. Fine tuning the pitch in a chord requires proper balance (volume relationships between parts) and, lastly, color matching. In the past, we called color matching *vowel matching*. Vowel matching gets you in the "ballpark," but true intonation in chord singing comes from the matching of resonance and vocal color. It is possible to lock and ring chords while actually singing different vowels if the resonance and color of such vowels are "complementary"—that is, work together to help the ear "tune."

The method I have developed and teach has three simple steps. (1) Pitches. (2) Word Sounds. (3) Integration. If you learn the pitches of your part on "loo" or "doo," you will accomplish some very important things that you would not accomplish if you had just plunged ahead the old way, attempting to learn notes and words at the same time.

Our brain is actually a big tape recorder. If you learn pitches first on "doo," some very interesting things begin to happen. First, there is nothing else for the brain to focus on other than the pitches and pitch patterns. There are no words, no changes from vowel to vowel, no changes in color or resonance, no consonants. Because we use the same sound over and over, "doo," we can sort of forget about it and focus on the pitches and pitch patterns. It is all those "other things" that complicate the learning process and that invariably cause us to go out of tune in very short order if they are attempted in the early learning stages or not applied with considerable skill.

If given a chance to focus on a single task, the brain will actually record the pitches, and they will remain in memory in the subconscious. A few times through the song, listening to a recording that has no words, just the pitch sung with "doo," is the simplest and easiest way for the subconscious to "record" the pitches of the song. If there are a few tricky places, just spend a little more time listening and "doo"-ing those places.

After a few times through on "doo," the pitches are recorded in the subconscious.

How do we know this? At first you have to trust, because it is difficult to accept the presence of things that we are not aware of. But that fact will soon be made clear enough. The next step is word sounds. To begin to master the flow of word sounds, we use a method called *silent audiation*. That is the process of "mouthing" the word sounds, the vowels, the consonants, the *m*s and *n*s as if you were performing the song. *But . . . you make no singing sound.* It is more than just saying the words silently, it is actually singing without making sound. You breathe, articulate consonants, form vowels shapes, keep the throat open, lift the palate, arch the tongue forward, place in the mask—that is, all the things you would do when you sing, but you make no sound. So, steps 1 and 2 are "doo"-ing pitches and silent audiation. You can do these steps separately, over and over, until you are ready to move to the last step. By doing so, you will be laying excellent groundwork for the final step . . . integration.

Before talking about integration, a word on silent audiation is in order. The purpose of this activity is to train the vocal muscles to memorize the flow and positions of the word sounds while actually hearing the pitch in your head. What makes one song different from another is the combination of pitches and how the phonetics flow. The elements of the performance are always the same. The same twelve pitches are used, maybe in a different key; words are composed of the same vowels and consonants. What is different is the order. That is what makes each song unique. So learning the order of events is 90 percent of the learning process. Silent audiation allows one to focus exclusively on the order of "events," from shape to shape, so that the muscles learn the vocal movements and learn to anticipate these movements as the pitches and word sounds flow along.

By doing this silently, it gives your brain a chance to associate the subconscious pitch with the muscle movement. That is very important, so I will say it again: *By doing this silently, it gives your brain a chance to associate the subconscious pitch with the muscle movement.*

Every vowel and its duration of sound is therefore associated with a pitch. If we hear it or can imagine it, the vocal mechanism will go through the process of preparing to sing. When we actually engage the mind and say "sing," the shape, if practiced, will be there and the pitch, if previously reviewed (with "doo"), will associate itself with the shape (i.e., the vowel).

Lanny Bansham, Olympic sharpshooter, the first to score a perfect 400 (all bullseyes) and to win the Olympic gold medal, was unable to go to the practice range to shoot six weeks before the Olympics. So to keep in shape, he practiced the motions of shooting "bullseyes" without firing a shot. He steadied himself, cleared his mind, aimed, squeezed the trigger, and imagined the perfect shot, every time. In that six-week period, he never even fired a rifle. At the Olympics, he just repeated what he had practiced "silently" before. Such is the nature of the mind, use of imagery, and training the muscle memory.

At first, you can practice word-sound flow listening to the pitches from our learning track, but eventually you will want to do silent audiation and attempt to hear the sounds of the pitches in your head. That's the *audiation* part . . . hearing in your head. As you practice, you will discover it is not that difficult. You have to use your imagination and memory, but the "doo" activity will provide a very strong experience from which to draw.

The integration part will actually be quite simple now. The pitches have been recorded in the subconscious. The muscle memory has been trained to shape and flow through the word sounds. As you now start to sing, you shouldn't be surprised to find the notes come booming forth from your subconscious as they are associated with the space and shapes of the vowels that you have already practiced.

I have watched many a singer struggle with poor learning habits; they often say, "I may be slow, but this is the way I learn." Too often they discover they learned many places incorrectly or sing many notes out of tune. The fact is that learning a song is not so much about learning notes and words as it is giving the pitches a "place to be heard." This method does just that.

It is my experience that singers using this method learn faster and more accurately. They maintain tonal center and sing more chords in tune. Please take advantage of our learning tracks that use computer-accurate tone generation on a "Doo Voice" sound that works in concert with this learning method. And please let us know if this method has been helpful to you with a testimonial.

Harmony Singers . . . a Special Tip for You

Spend as much time at first listening to the lead part as well as your own. It's right there on your learning track. Ultimately, your harmony part is tuned to the "anticipated" melody line. So you need to know where the lead is going. (Of course, it helps if the lead actually "gets there.")

Don't learn your part as melody from note to note. A harmony part sung "independently" from the melody will tend to sound out of tune. "Doo" the pitches so that you learn the note patterns. And practice silent audiation to get the muscle memory activated. But then the integration process for you is one of listening to the melody as you sing your harmony part, allowing your ear to make the fine-tuning adjustments. On the learning track, when you are ready, flip the balance to the right speaker all the way so that you can't hear your part in the left speaker. Then listen and sing along with the other three, and you'll get some good experience in tuning.

Have fun singing . . . have more fun singing in tune!

APPENDIX G
Barbershop Humor

Barbershoppers love to sing, and they love to enjoy fellowship, camaraderie, and good fun. As might be expected, through the years distinct identities and stereotypes have grown up around the four vocal parts in the barbershop world. It is true that some good singers may be able to sing more than one part, but every singer is loyal to the part he or she is singing at the time. Thus, it happens that jokes are often made about the four barbershop parts, just as in an orchestra one hears viola and bassoon jokes, and in opera one hears soprano and tenor jokes.

Who are the leads? They are often jokingly portrayed as egotistical attention-seekers, since they have the melody and therefore are apt to think they are the main show. "Q: How does a lead change a light bulb? A: He just holds the bulb and the world revolves around him."[1] Sometimes it is implied that leads are not smart enough to sing a harmony part but can only sing the familiar melody. "Have you ever tried to teach a lead three measures of music in which he is asked to give up the melody line?"[2] Or "Q: How do you tell when your lead singer is at the door? A: He can't find the key and doesn't know when to come in."[3]

In the tenor world, female tenors are often portrayed as ditsy "airheads"—people whose brains have been affected by singing all those high notes. Male tenors are often teased about singing too loud, especially if they are true tenors who have a strong mixed vocal registration. "The talent of a tenor is inversely proportionate to the weight of his music bag."[4] Or "If you took all the tenors in the world and laid them end to end . . . it would be a good idea."[5]

Basses are teased about being laid-back people, interested in comfort. Jokes may include references of "real men" or "real women" singing bass, or they may imply that basses are lazy or not very bright. "The bass section: never needlessly disturb a thing at rest."[6] Or "Why are barbershop show intermissions limited to twenty minutes? So they don't have to retrain the bass section."[7]

The baritones are seen as the anal-retentive types, attentive to detail and keeping everyone else in line. "If there is a nit to be picked, bet on the baritone to do it."[8] Or "Q: What's the difference between a lawn mower and a baritone? A: You can tune the lawn mower."[9]

Singers of each part are quick to assert that the music would not be barbershop without their own "most important part," and the truth is that they are all correct. You can't sing barbershop alone!

Not all barbershop jokes are related to the individual parts, of course. Some are simply about music, singing, or barbershop life in general, such as this one from former Barbershop Harmony Society CEO Ed Watson: "Q: How many barbershoppers does it take to change a light bulb? A: Five—one to change it and four to sing about how much they miss the old one." Here are a few more examples from Bill Gibbons's collection of one-liners:

> "The older you get, the better your voice used to be."
> "There is too much apathy in most chapters—but who cares?"
> "God has given man the seemingly infinite capacity to remember countless tags plus one of the chapter chorus contest songs."
> "Wear white pants to all chorus rehearsals. No one will ever ask you to help with the risers."
> "The easiest way to find your misplaced pitch pipe is to buy a new one."
> "No matter how many rooms in the headquarters hotel, the guy who starts up his car at 5 a.m. is always parked under your window."
> "Barbershoppers will accept your idea much more readily if you tell them that last year's championship quartet/chorus did it that way."

"Contests: You have six minutes to make history or be history."

"Show Chairman: No one ever left the theater of an annual show saying, 'It was a lousy show, but it did come in under budget.'"

"There is a pessimist in your chapter who thinks the old days were better. You know who I mean. You also know the optimist who believes that things are getting better. Trust me on this one, they're both wrong."

"When a barbershopper tells you, 'I'm as good a singer as you are,' it means that he thinks he is better."

"Judges who think they know everything about barbershopping are very irritating to those of us who do."

"Contest Tip: Make sure that your two songs were originally arranged on parchment."

"A 'totally fair' contest is a winners' definition."

"I sang lead in a high school quartet. After our first public performance my mother suggested that I find three other kids who didn't sharp so often. Mothers are wonderful."

"A wise man once told me that to grow, I should 'meet regularly with those who hold vastly different views than I did.' Could that be your director's motivation?"

"Quiz: If one were to stand up in the Saturday-night audience of the next International Contest and shout 'You're flat!' would he be:
  (a) subject to protection under the first amendment (free speech)
  (b) subject to prosecution under the fifth amendment (conspiring to riot)
  (c) appointed as Chairman of Judges at the next International Contest."

"I asked our director if I could sing a solo while the chorus hummed in the background. He asked what my other two wishes were."

"In every barbershop chapter, there will always be one person who knows what is going on. Get rid of him."

"A guaranteed way to increase chorus membership—go out and buy new risers that meet your current needs."[10]

In the decade of the 1990s, Kira Prewitt Wagner amassed a collection of personal stories or vignettes from various Sweet Adelines around the world and published these tales in a little book titled *But Honey, It's*

Only One Night a Week (and Other Likely Stories). Here are a couple of accounts that give a little taste of what it is like to be a barbershopper.

> Being a new Sweet Adeline, I was so excited to be going to my first International in Toronto, Canada. I called my father back on the east coast and told him that I was going to Canada, and he inquired whether I would be able to see the Queen, since she was touring with her son Prince Charles. I told him that I didn't believe so, since I would be busy elsewhere. Later on I was looking through *The Pitch Pipe*, and in the schedule of events it listed the Queen's reception; and knowing that Queen Elizabeth was to be in the same area, I was so impressed that she would be attending a Sweet Adeline Convention. In preparation I packed a formal but modest gown and long gloves so I would be properly dressed. I must have told everyone I knew that I was going to meet the Queen. It was during Halloween time, and there were many events tied into this, including a costume parade and the precursor to the Coronet Club Show, a parade of former champion quartets topped off by Renee Craig and the Cracker Jills singing their poignant Judy at the Palace package. Then came the quartet finals where four lovely ladies from the northwest, The Sea-Adelines, were crowned quartet champions. Imagine my surprise when I attended the Queen's reception and met not one Queen of England, but our own four Queens of Harmony! (Jean O'Neill, Pacific Empire Chorus)[11]

> We had been at a regional meeting and learned a new song. During the trip back home, we stopped for some food at a rest stop on the Florida Turnpike. While standing in line to pay for our food, the tenor and I had gotten separated by a "civilian" (non–Sweet Adeline). Beth was singing the new song we had learned in her tenor part. When she paid for her food and left the line, the woman that was standing between us turned to me and said, "Poor dear, she's as tone-deaf as can be." (Pat Evens, Thursday Night Live Quartet/Gainesville Chorus)[12]

Never let it be said that barbershoppers do not know how to have a good time. The ability to sing and the ability to laugh go hand in hand.

NOTES

1. Dick Johnson, *Barbershop Jokes*, 2, accessed January 29, 2016, http://probeweb.org/BulletinEditors/BEHumor/morebari.htm.

2. Bill Gibbons, *One-Liners*, 5, accessed January 29, 2016, http://probeweb.org/BulletinEditors/BE-Fillers/moreoners.htm.
3. *Vocal Jokes*, 1, accessed January 29, 2016, www.ahajokes.com/vocal.html.
4. Gibbons, *One Liners*, 4.
5. Gibbons, *One Liners*, 7.
6. Gibbons, *One Liners*, 2.
7. Gibbons, *One Liners*, 7.
8. Gibbons, *One Liners*, 5.
9. Johnson, *Barbershop Jokes*, 1.
10. Gibbons, *One Liners*, 1–7.
11. Kira Prewitt Wagner, *But Honey, It's Only One Night a Week (and Other Likely Stories)* (Napa Valley, CA: XXX, 1995), 36.
12. Wagner, *But Honey*, 67.

BIBLIOGRAPHY

Wagner, Kira Prewitt. *But Honey, It's Only One Night a Week (and Other Likely Stories)*. Napa Valley, CA: 1995.

INDEX

abdominal muscles, 16, *17*, *18*
abduction, 20
ACAAI. *See* American College of Allergy, Asthma, and Immunology
a cappella, 57, 59–60, 131–32, 133
A Cappella Harmony Academy (AHA), 116
ACDA. *See* American Choral Directors Association
ACJ. *See* approved candidate judge
acoustics, 13, 72. *See also* vocal science
Adam's apple. *See* larynx
adduction, 20
Adeline. *See* Sweet Adelines International
ad lib, 133
African Americans, 2, 3
afterglow, 133
AHA. *See* A Cappella Harmony Academy

AHSOW. *See* Ancient and Harmonious Society of Woodshedders
alcohol, 46
alignment, 70–71, 173
alveoli, 14
American Choral Directors Association (ACDA), 127
American College of Allergy, Asthma, and Immunology (ACAAI), 36
Ancient and Harmonious Society of Woodshedders (AHSOW), 133
Anderson, Edna Mae, 9
ANS. *See* autonomic nervous system
approved candidate judge (ACJ), 119–20
areas (barbershop organizational units), 114–15, 133
arrangement devices, 133. *See also* embellishments; swipe

arrangements, 56–58, 85, 122, 133; for tuning perfect fifths, 97, 166, 167–71
arrangers, 121–22, 133
Arrangers Manual (Sweet Adelines International), 121
articulation, 13, 28, 29–30, 173, 174
arytenoids, 21, *22*
Association of eXtreme Quartetting Harmony Brigades, Inc., 124
the Atlantic University Quartet, *2*
attack, 133, 134, 136, 138
audiation, 68, 96, 99, 134, 181, 182, 183
auditions, 67–69
augmented triads, *56*
autonomic nervous system (ANS), 41

BABS. *See* British Association of Barbershop Singers
balance, 70, 71, 134. *See also* chord balancing; mix
balanced phonation, 72–73
Balk, H. Wesley, 100–102
ballad, 59, 134
Bansham, Lanny, 181–82
barbershop. *See specific topics*
Barbershop Arranging Manual (Barbershop Harmony Society), 56–57
Barbershop B&B CouchSurfing, 131
Barbershop Harmony Society (BHS), 4, 12, 81, 134; arranger education opportunities in, 121–22; *Barbershop Arranging Manual* by, 56–57; choruses in, 8–9; competitions of, 104–5, 108, 123; education of directors by, 115–16, 117; education offered by, 111, 114–15; harmony brigades of, 124; Harmony University of, 115–16, 117, 127; judge certification in, 118–19; music educator outreach by, 127; race discrimination in, 11; youth programs of, 125, 126. *See also* Mixed Barbershop Harmony Association; Society for the Propagation and Encouragement of Barber Shop Quartet Singing in America
barbershop-ninth chords (dominant-ninth chords), *54*, 55
barbershop organizations: lifetime membership in, 130; music educator outreach by, 126–27; music publishing by, 85; youth programs of, 125, 126. *See also* Ancient and Harmonious Society of Woodshedders; area; Barbershop Harmony Society; British Association of Barbershop Singers; chapter; competitions; district; division; Harmony, Incorporated; international; Ladies Association of British Barbershop Singers; Mixed Barbershop Harmony Association; region; Society for the Propagation and Encouragement of Barber Shop Quartet Singing in America; Sweet Adelines International
barbershop organizations, educational offerings of, 111, 114; for arrangers, 121–22; barbershop competitions as, 108, 109–10, 122–23; for directors, 115–16, 117–18; international schools of, 115–16; Internet resources for, 116; judge certification and, 118–21. *See also* coaching

INDEX

barbershop-seventh chords (dominant-seventh chords) (major-minor seventh chords), 54, 55, 97, 134, 140
barbershop sound, 134
barbershop style, 134; arrangements in, 56; chord balancing in, 53, 92; chords of, eleven, 54, 55, 56; embellishments in, 60, *61*, 62, *63*, 137; historical changes of, 4–5, 6, 7; performance requirements for, 48; rhythm and tempo in, 58–59; song form in, 57–58; song types in, 58–59; vocal challenge of, 77; vowel matching in, 53, 92–93, 174, 180. *See also* four parts, in barbershop; lock and ring; tuning, in barbershop style
bari. *See* baritone
bari cherry, 61, 134
baritone (bari), 52, 76, 84, 134, 174, 186
the Bartlesville Barflies, 5, 103
bass, 52, 76, 84, 96–97, 134, 175, 186; chord balancing and, 53
beat, 94, 134, 142
bell chords, *61*, 134
belting, 134
BHS. *See* Barbershop Harmony Society
BinG! Barbershop, 12
bird's eye (fermata), 137
blending, 94
body language (gestures), 101–2, 138
Bonney, Al, 124
Boyle's Law, 14
brat, barbershop, 134
breathing. *See* pulmonary system
breath management, 71–72, 89–90
breath support, 18–19

British Association of Barbershop Singers (BABS), 12
the Buffalo Bills, 5, 6, 7
But Honey, It's Only One Night a Week (and Other Likely Stories) (Wagner), 187–88

caesura (railroad tracks), 142
career, 113
cartilages, of larynx, 21, *22*
cascade, 135
Cash, Owen C., 3–4
Cazden, Joanna, 40
CCM. *See* Contemporary Commercial Music
certification: of competition judges, 118–21; of directors, 117–18
chapter (barbershop organizational unit), 82, 118, 130–31, 135
charts. *See* arrangements
chestnut, 135
chest voice, 23, 74, 75, 135
chord, bust a, 49, 63–64, 135. *See also* lock and ring
chord balancing: bass and, 53; for lock and ring, 92
The Chordbuster's March (Wyatt), 63–64
chorditorium, 135
chords, 135, 138, 139, 144, 145, 166; barbershop seventh, 54, 55, 97, 134, 140; of barbershop style, eleven, 54, 55, 56; lock and ring, overtones and, 51–52. *See also* bell chords
chords, vocal. *See* vocal folds
choreography, 70, 78, 91
choruses, 8–9, 81, 82, 86–87, 104. *See also specific choruses*
chromatic, 135

cigarettes, 46
circle of fifths, 135, 166
Clark, Diane, 79
climax, 135
closed voicing (close harmony), 135
coaching, 102, 108, 112, 113, 135
Collegiate Quartet Competition, 126
color, 135. *See also* timbre
color chords, 135
color matching, 180
combination tone, 135
comedic, 135
Common Practice Period, 64n2
competitions, 12; BHS and, 104–5, 108, 123; choruses in, 104; as educational offerings, 108, 109–10, 122–23; of HI, 108, 123; Internet resources for, 123; repertoire for, 59; of SAI, 9, *10*, 11, 105, 106–8, 123; solidarity in, 108, 109–10; of SPEBSQSA, 103; for youth, 126. *See also* World Mixed Harmony Competition
competitions, judging, 103; categories for, 102, 104–5, 106–7; certification for, 118–21
complete chords, 135
Conable, Barbara, 67
coning, 135
consonance, 136
construction, 136. *See also* form, song
contemporary commercial music (CCM), 77, 114, 136
Contest & Judging Manual (Barbershop Harmony Society), 104–5
cool-downs. *See* vocal cool-downs
cps. *See* cycles per second
the Cracker Jills, *10*

Craig, Renee, 10
A Crash Course in Vocal Production (Clark), 79
crescendo, 90–91, 136
cricothyroid (CT) muscles, 22, 23, 74, 75
cross-training, vocal, 47
CT. *See* cricothyroid muscles
culture: of barbershop, 129–31, 132; divisions of, 3
cycles per second (cps), 45, 94, 138. *See also* Hertz

DCP. *See* Director Certification Program
the Decaturettes, *105*
decrescendo, 136
diaphragm, 14, *15*, 16, 71
diatonic, 136
diatonic scale, 136
difference tone, 136
diminished-seventh chords, 56
diminuendo, 136
diphthong, 136
Director Certification Program (DCP), 117–18
directors, 67–68, 69, 89, 102, 127, 175; educational offerings for, 115–16, 117–18
Directors First, 118
dissonance, 136
district (barbershop organizational unit), 105, 114–15, 136
division (barbershop organizational unit), 105, 107
divisions (cultural), 3
divorced tone, 136
divorced voicing, 136
dominant-ninth chords (barbershop-ninth chords), *54*, 55

dominant-seventh chords (barbershop-seventh chords) (major-minor seventh chords), 54, 55, 97, 134, 140
"Down Our Way" (barbershop polecat), 96–97
dramatic skills, 78. *See also* body language; facial expressions; showmanship category, in SAI competitions
drugs, 37–38, 39, 46
dynamics, 137

echo, 61, 137
education. *See* barbershop organizations, educational offerings of; coaching; learning, of new songs; personal vocal instruction; voice teachers
educators, barbershop organization outreach to, 126–27
elastic recoil, 16
e-mail discussion groups, 131
embellishments, 60, *61*, 62, *63*, 137
Emmons, Shirlee, 40
emotions, 100–102
energy, 137
enharmonic, 137
Entertainer's Secret, 34
environmental irritants, 46
epiglottis, 21
epithelium, *20*, 21
everglow, 137
expanded sound, 137
expression category, in SAI competitions, 106–7
external oblique muscles, 17, *18*

Facebook, 131
facial expressions, 78, 101, 173

falsetto (head voice), *23*, 74, 75, 137, 139
family, in barbershop, 130–31, 132. *See also* solidarity, in barbershop competitions
Fenton Lakes Chorus, 87
fermata (bird's eye), 137
fifths, 54, 64n2, 135, 137, 141, 165; tuning of, 96–97, 166, *167–71*
fifth wheel, 137
flat seventh, 137
float, 137
flow, 137
focus, mental, 47, 174, 180
focused singing, 174
For Heaven's Sake Quartet, *109*
form, song, 57–58, 137
formants, 25, *26*, 27, 138
forte, 138
fortissimo, 138
forward motion, 60, 90–91, 138
Foster, Stephen, 1–2
four-part chords, 138
four parts, in barbershop, 52, 84–85, 99, 174, 185–86; vocal techniques for, 76–77. *See also* baritone; bass; lead; tenor
fraternities, singing, 130
free style, 138
frequency. *See* cycles per second
fullness, 138
fundamental, 23, 44, 138

gang singing, 138
gargle, 36
gastroesophageal reflux (GERD), 38–39
gender: in arrangements, 58; barbershop song types and, 59; in harmony brigades, 124; mixed

harmony and, 11–12; vocal science and, 20, 27; vocal wellness and, 44, 45. *See also* Harmony, Incorporated; Sweet Adelines International
genre. *See* barbershop style
GERD. *See* gastroesophageal reflux
gestures (body language), 101–2, 138
Gibbons, Bill, 186–87
glimmer, 138
glissando, 138
glottis, 20, *23*; attack and release of, 138; pressure below, 143
the Great Lakes Chorus, 8, 104
growth, 175

H2. *See* histamine blockers
half step, 138
Hall, Rupert, 3–4
harmonic, 24, 138
harmonic movement, 138
harmonic series, 23, *24*, 138
harmonization, 138
harmony, 139, 165. *See also specific topics*
Harmony, Incorporated (HI), 139; barbershop competitions of, 108, 123; in barbershop history, 11; director education opportunities in, 118; education and, 111, 114–15; judge certification in, 120–21; youth programs of, 125, 126
harmony brigades, 123–24
Harmony Explosion (youth program), 125
Harmony for Young Women (youth program), 125
Harmony Foundation International, 126

the Harmony Halls, 5, *6*
Harmony Platoon, 124
Harmony University, 115–16, 117, 127
head voice (falsetto), *23*, 74, 75, 137, 139
health. *See* mental wellness; vocal wellness
Hertz (Hz), 23, 139
HI. *See* Harmony, Incorporated
Hicks, Val, 96–97, 165–66, *167–71*
histamine (H2) blockers, 39
history, of barbershop, 1; African American roots of, *2*, 3; barbershop competitions in, 9, *10*, 11, 103–4; BHS in, 4, 8–9; choruses in, 8–9; cultural divisions crossed in, 3; HI in, 11; SPEBSQSA in, 3–4, 103; style changes in, 4–5, *6*, *7*; Sweet Adelines International in, 9, *10*, 11
hobby, performance conflict with, 129–30
home remedies, 36–37
homophony/homophonic, 54, 139
honey, 36
horizontal tuning, 139
How to Use Your Classical Training with Barbershop Harmony (Vaughn), 77
Humidflyer, 35
humor, barbershop, 185–88
hydration, 33–36, 44
hyoid bone, 29
hyperhidrosis (overhydration), 34
Hz. *See* Hertz

IES. *See* International Education Symposium

INDEX

imagery, 181–82
IMAP. *See* Sweet Adelines International Music Arrangers Program
implied harmony, 139
incomplete chords, 139
inflection, 139
inharmonic overtones, 24
inline singing. *See* resonance matching; vowel matching
Instant Classic, 73–74, 94
intensity, 139
intercostal muscles, 16, *17*
international (barbershop organizational unit), 139
International Education Symposium (IES), 77, 116, 118
international schools, 115–16
international stage, barbershop on, 12
Internet resources: for arrangements, 122; for barbershop competitions, 123; for barbershop culture, 131; for barbershop organization education, 116; for coaching, 112; for drugs and vocal wellness, 37; for nutrition and vocal wellness, 33; for personal vocal instruction, 114; for vocal science, 30
interpolation, 139
interpretation, 139
interval, 139
intonation, 97, 139, 140
intro, 60, 139
inversion: first, 137; second, 143

Joplin, Scott, 3
judges. *See* competitions, judging

Judging Category Description Book (Sweet Adelines International), 105, 106–7
just intonation, 97, 140

Keller, Kevin, 56, 58
key, 140
key change, 62, 140
Kitzmiller, Scott, 73–74

Ladies Association of British Barbershop Singers (LABBS), 12
lamina propria, *20*, 21
laryngitis, 21
laryngopharyngeal reflux (LPR), 38–39
larynx, 19, 24, 140; cartilages of, 21, 22; drugs, mucous and, 37–38, 46; hydration, mucous and, 33–34; injury to, 31–32, 45; timbre of, 23; vocal folds of, *20*, 21, 32, 45, 145. *See also* glottis
latissimi dorsi muscles, 19
Lawrence, Van, 33
lead, 52, 76, 84, 95–96, 140, 174, 185; song learning and, 182–83
leading tone, 97, 140
learning, of new songs, 99, 177, 178–81, 182–83
LeBorgne, Wendy, 67, 70
legato, 140
Lewellen, Christina, 123
lifetime membership, 130
listening, 96, 178–79
lock and ring, 58, 91, 140, 179–80; chord balancing for, 92; chords, overtones and, 51–52
loudness, 140
LoVetri, Jeanette, 75

LPR. *See* laryngopharyngeal reflux
lungs. *See* pulmonary system
Lyne, Greg, 173
lyrical, 140
lyrics, 57, 100, 140, 180–81

major-minor seventh chords (dominant-seventh chords) (barbershop-seventh chords), 54, 55, 97, 134, 140
major-ninth chords, 55
major scales, 58, 140
major seventh, 140
major-seventh chords, 55
major-sixth chords, 55
major triads, 51, 54, 55
marcato, 140
MBHA. *See* Mixed Barbershop Harmony Association
medications. *See* drugs
medley, 140
Meiser, Patsy, 125
melody, 62, 140
mental wellness, 40–41, 47
meter, 59, 140
mezzo forte, 140
mezzo piano, 140
migration, 140
mind. *See* mental wellness
Minor Chords (youth program), 126
minor scale, 58
minor-seventh chords, 55
minor-sixth chords, 55
minor triads, 55
mix, 75, 140
Mixed Barbershop Harmony Association (MBHA), 12
mixed harmony, 11–12
modes, 22, 23. *See also* projective modes; registers

modification, 141
Monteith, Cory, 46
MPA. *See* musical performance anxiety
mucous, 33–34, 37–38, 44, 46
muscles: of articulation, 29–30; cricothyroid, 22, 23, 74, 75; of pulmonary system, 14, *15*, 16, *17*, *18*, 19; silent audiation and, 181–82, 183; thyroarytenoid, 21, 22, 23, 74, 75. *See also* diaphragm; larynx
musical instruments, 13, 72
musicality, 141
musical performance anxiety (MPA), 40–41
music category, in barbershop competitions, 104, 106
The Music Man (Willson), 6
music publishing, 85

National Association for Music Education (NAfME), 126–27
National Association of Teachers of Singing (NATS), 30, 37, 114, 127
National Center for Voice and Speech (NCVS), 30, 37
NATS. *See* National Association of Teachers of Singing
NCVS. *See* National Center for Voice and Speech
Neti pots, 35–36
neurology, 29–30, 41
Newman, Jennifer, 124
ninth chords, *54*, 55
notes, 141, 180–81
nutrition, 32–33

octave, 96, 141
Oklahoma, barbershop history in, 3

INDEX

Open the Doors Youth Chorus, *126*
opera, 26, 27
Operations Manual (Association of eXtreme Quartetting Harmony Brigades, Inc.), 124
overhydration (hyperhidrosis), 34
overtones, 23, 24, 141; lock and ring, chords and, 51–52. *See also* chord balancing

parallel fifths, 54, 64n2, 141
part, 141
partials, 141
patter, 62, 141
pause/grand pause, 141
peel-off, 62, 141
perfect fifths, 97, 165, 166, *167–71*
performance, 141; barbershop style requirements for, 48; BHS competition category of, 104; hobby conflict with, 129–30; MPA and, 40–41; psychologists specializing in, 40
personal vocal instruction (PVI), 113–14, 142
pharynx, 33–34, 93, 141
phonation, 20, 21, 72–73
phonation threshold pressure (PTP), 34
phrasing, 141
physical exercise, 39–40
pianissimo, 141
pick-up quartet, 141
ping, 6–7, 141
Pitch Perfect (movie), 131
Pitch Perfect 2 (movie), 131
pitch pipe, 141
polecat, 96–97, 141
polyphony/polyphonic, 141
portamento, 142

post, 62, *63*, 142
posture. *See* alignment
Power Performance for Singers: Transcending the Barriers (Emmons and Thomas), 40
PPI. *See* proton pump inhibitors
practice strategies, for vocal wellness, 46–47. *See also* rehearsals; songs, learning new
precision, 142
preglow, 142
presentation, 142
projective modes, 100–102, 142
props, 142
proton pump inhibitors (PPI), 39
psycho-behavioral therapy, 40
psychologists, performance, 40
PTP. *See* phonation threshold pressure
pulmonary system, 14, *15*, 16, *17*, *18*, 19
pulse beat, 142
punch line, 142
push beat, 142
PVI. *See* personal vocal instruction
Pythagorean comma, 142
Pythagorean tuning, 142

quartets, 81, 82, 98–99, 141. *See also* four parts, in barbershop; very large quartet; *specific quartets*
Queens of Harmony, 10

race discrimination, 11
railroad tracks (caesura), 142
range, vocal, 74–76. *See also* registers; tessitura
rectus abdominus muscles, 16, *17*, *18*
reflux, 38–39
regions (barbershop organizational units), 114–15, 142

registers, 22, 142; CT muscles, TA muscles and, 23, 74, 75; glottis configurations in, 23; vocal techniques for, 74–75. *See also* chest voice; head voice
rehearsals, 48, 85, 86, 95–96, 99, 175. *See also* learning, of new songs
release, 142; of glottis, 138
repertoire, 59
resonance, 13, 24, 142; riser placement and, 97–98; spectrum analyzer for, 27–28; in vocal tract, 25–26; vowel matching and, 92–93, 174, 180. *See also* formants
resonance matching, 73–74
"Resonating with Instant Classic" (Kitzmiller), 73–74
resonators, 13, 25, 93, 143
rest, 143
rhinosinusitis, 35–36
rhythm, 58–59, 143
ring, 6, 7, 143. *See also* lock and ring
riser buddy, 68, 130, 143
riser placement, 97–98
Rising Star Quartet Contest, 126
root, 143
root position, 143
Rosenberg, Marci, 67, 70
rubato, 143

SAI. *See* Sweet Adelines International
saltwater, 35, 36
scales, 58, 136, 140, 143, 144
scholarships, 118, 126, 127
scissors, 143
SCJC. *See* Society Contest & Judging Committee
the Sea-Adelines, 188
sets, 143

seventh chords, 54, 55, 56, 97, 134, 140
sevenths, 97, 137, 140, 143
Sharon, Deke, 131–32
sheet music. *See* arrangements
showmanship category, in SAI competitions, 107
singing, 14, 27–28. *See also* vocal athletes
singing category, in BHS competitions, 104–5
sixth, 143
sixth chords, 55
smoking, 46
social media, 131
Society Contest & Judging Committee (SCJC), 119
Society for the Propagation and Encouragement of Barber Shop Quartet Singing in America (SPEBSQSA), 3–4, 81, 103
software, 27–28
solidarity, in barbershop competitions, 108, 109–10
solo passages, 62
Somatic Voicework—the LoVetri Method, 75
songs, 57–59, 137, 143; learning new, 99, 177, 178–81, 182–83. *See also* arrangements
sound, of musical instruments, 13, 72. *See also* barbershop sound; expanded sound; unit sound; vocal science
sound category, in SAI competitions, 106
SPEBSQSA. *See* Society for the Propagation and Encouragement of Barber Shop Quartet Singing in America

INDEX

spectrum analyzer, 27–28
speech, 44–45, 75. *See also* National Center for Voice and Speech
staccato, 143
stage presence, 143
Standard American English, 53, 91–92
standing order, 98–99. *See also* riser placement
steam inhalers, 34–35
style. *See* barbershop style
subconscious, 180–81
subglottal pressure, 143
success, embodying, 175
sum tone, 143
the Suntones, 7, 8
Sweet Adelines International (SAI), 143; barbershop competitions of, 9, *10*, 11, 105, 106–8, 123; in *But Honey, It's Only One Night a Week (and Other Likely Stories)*, 187–88; *A Crash Course in Vocal Production* for, 79; director education opportunities in, 117–18; education and, 111, 114–15; International Education Symposium of, 77, 116, 118; on international stage, 12; judge certification in, 119–20; judging categories of, 105, 106–7; music educator outreach and, 127; race discrimination in, 11; travel opportunities and, 125; youth programs of, 125, 126
Sweet Adelines International Music Arrangers Program (IMAP), 121–22
swing tune, 59, 144
swipe, 60, *61*, 144
synchronization, 54, 144
syncopation, 144

TA. *See* thyroarytenoid muscle
tag, 57–58, 60, 144
teas, 34, 36
temperament, 137, 144, 145
tempo, 58–59, 144
tenor, 52, 84–85, 144, 174, 185–86; vocal technique for, 76
tension, 29
tenuto, 144
tessitura, 74, 144
theme, 144
third, 97, 144
third inversion chords, 144
Thomas, Alma, 40
3-D system of vowels, 93
throat singers, 24
thyroarytenoid (TA) muscle, 21, 22, 23, 74, 75
thyroid cartilage, 21
timbre, 22–23, 98, 135, 144
time, nonsinging, 141
timing, 144
tonal center, 144
tone. *See* combination tone; difference tone; divorced tone
tone color, 135. *See also* timbre
tonic, 144
tonic chords, 145
travel opportunities, 125
tremolo, 145
triads, 51, *54*, *55*, *56*, 81
trills, 73
tritone, 145
Tropical Harmony Chorus, 125
Tulsa (Oklahoma), barbershop history in, 3, 4, 9, 103, 105
tuning, in barbershop style, 56–57; of fifths, 96–97, 166, *167–71*; song learning and, 179–80, 183; unison and, 94; vocal techniques

for, 95–97, 166, *167–71*. See also horizontal tuning; intonation; lock and ring; Pythagorean tuning; temperament
turn-around, 62
Tuva, 24
TVF. *See* the Voice Foundation

unison, 61–62, 94
unit sound, 89
uptune, 58–59, 145

vacuum, 14
Vaughn, Kim, 77
vertical tuning, 145
very large quartet (VLQ), 145
vibrato, 77, 145
vinegar, apple cider, 36–37
Visualization for Singers (Cazden), 40
VLQ. *See* very large quartet
The Vocal Athlete (LeBorgne and Rosenberg), 67, 70
vocal athletes, 31, 32, 39–41, 42–43, 47
vocal challenge, of barbershop style, 77
vocal chords. *See* vocal folds
vocal color, 135. *See also* timbre
vocal cool-downs, 44
vocal fitness programs, 43–44
vocal folds, *20*, 21, 32, 45, 145. *See also* registers
vocal hygiene, 41
vocal injury, 31–32, 42, 45
vocal intensity (volume), 45, 145
vocalises, 44, 73
vocal ligament, 20, 21
vocal longevity, 42–43
vocal naps, 45, 48
vocal science, 13, 20, 27, 30; of balanced phonation, 72–73.

See also articulation; larynx; pulmonary system; resonance; vocal tract
vocal techniques: for alignment, 70–71, 173; auditions and, 67–69; for balanced phonation, 72–73; breath management in, 71–72; dramatic skills and, 78; for four barbershop parts, 76–77; reading recommendations for, 67; for resonance matching, 73–74; style-specific challenges of, 77; for tuning, 95–97, 166, *167–71*; for vocal range, 74–76. *See also* vocal cool-downs; vocal warm-ups
vocal tract, 24, 25–26, 27–28
vocal warm-ups, 43–44; for tuning perfect fifths, 97, 166, *167–71*
vocal wellness, 48, 49; drugs and, 37–38; environmental irritants and, 46; gender and, 44, 45; home remedies for, 36–37; hydration for, 33–34; nutrition for, 32–33; physical exercise and, 39–40; practice strategies for, 46–47; reflux and, 38–39; speech and, 44–45; vocal fitness programs for, 43–44; voice disorders and, 42. *See also* vocal injury; vocal longevity
voice, 23, *24*, 101. *See also* chest voice; head voice; range, vocal; speech
voice box. *See* larynx
voice disorders, 42
the Voice Foundation (TVF), 30
voice leading, 145
voice part. *See* part
Voices Incorporated Chorus, 83
voice teachers, 69, 89; auditions and, 68. *See also* National Association

of Teachers of Singing; personal vocal instruction
voicing, 135, 136, 143, 145
volume (vocal intensity), 45, 145
vowel matching, 53, 92–93, 174, 180
vowels: articulation positions of, 28, 173; in breath management exercise, 72; formant ranges for, 26, 27; for lock and ring, 52, 91–92; in register balance exercises, 74; in resonance matching exercise, 73–74; Standard American English and, 53, 91–92; 3-D system of, 93

Wagner, Kira Prewitt, 187–88
warm-ups. *See* vocal warm-ups

Watson, Ed, 186
wellness. *See* mental wellness; vocal wellness
What Every Musician Needs to Know about the Body (Conable), 67
whole step, 145
Willson, Meredith, 6, 129
Winehouse, Amy, 46
Women's Harmony Brigade, 124. *See also* gender
woodshedding, 145. *See also* Ancient and Harmonious Society of Woodshedders
World Mixed Harmony Competition, 12

youth programs, 125, 126

ABOUT THE AUTHORS

Diane M. Clark is a native of Memphis, Tennessee, where she received her early education in the Memphis City Schools. She earned high school certificates in voice and piano from the Rhodes Music Academy and received the bachelor of music degree with distinction from Rhodes College in 1962. Her first career was as director of Christian education and director of youth and children's choirs for Presbyterian churches in Birmingham and Mobile, Alabama.

In 1968, Clark received the master of music degree in voice pedagogy from Indiana University in Bloomington, and she began her university teaching career at Texas Tech University in Lubbock, where she taught for three years. In 1975, Clark joined the faculty at Rhodes College in Memphis, where she taught for thirty-two years. In 1980, she received the doctor of arts degree in music from the University of Mississippi in Oxford. In 2006, she retired as associate professor emerita of music at Rhodes.

Clark currently resides in Traverse City, Michigan, where she has a private voice studio and is adjunct voice faculty at Northwestern Michigan College. In 2013, she served as vocal director for the Old Town Playhouse production of *Les Misérables*. As a singer, Clark has been heard in recital, oratorio, music theatre, vocal jazz, and barbershop. She was a professional church musician for thirty-six years. She is a member of the National Association for Music Education (NAfME) and the

Somatic Voicework Teachers Association and has been a member of the National Association of Teachers of Singing (NATS) for almost fifty years. She was founding president of the Memphis Chapter of NATS and served two terms as Tennessee governor.

In 1992, as faculty coach for the Woolsocks men's barbershop ensemble at Rhodes, Clark joined Sweet Adelines International to learn more about barbershop. She was a member of the Memphis City Sound Chorus for ten years and its associate director for five. In Heart of Dixie Region 23, she was a regional coach and faculty member and served as education coordinator and coordinator of the Director Certification Program. For ten years, she was a Sweet Adelines international faculty member and taught several times at the International Education Symposium. In 2005 and 2006, she sang with the Metro Nashville Chorus, who were international champions in the Harmony Classic Small Chorus Division in 2006.

That same year Clark moved to Traverse City, Michigan, to become director of the Grand Traverse Show Chorus of Sweet Adelines. In Border Lakes Region 2, she is a regional coach and faculty member and serves as arrangers coordinator. In 2017, she became director of the Cherry Capital Men's Chorus of the Barbershop Harmony Society.

Billy J. Biffle was born and raised in Lubbock, Texas, the third son in a musical family. His mother and father were amateur musicians who instilled a love of music in all their sons. Biffle participated in choir and band all through school, including his time at North Texas State University and Texas Tech University, from which he received a bachelor of arts degree in 1969. He played trumpet all the way through school but put the horn aside after graduation. Some thirty-five years later, Biffle resumed playing the trumpet and now plays in three jazz bands in his hometown of Albuquerque, New Mexico, and leads the Barbershop All-Star Dixieland Band, which is a highlight of every Barbershop Harmony Society convention.

Biffle has been a barbershopper for over forty years and in that time has done just about everything a barbershopper can do. He directed the Albuquerque Chapter chorus for twenty years, winning four Rocky Mountain District championships and appearing in four international competitions. He has continually sung in quartets, winning two district championships, two senior district championships, and competing in two international competitions and one senior international competition. He was certified as a contest judge in the sound category in 1981 and the singing category in 1992 after having served on the leadership team that created the latter. Following more than twenty years of service, he was awarded judge emeritus status in 2007. He is also a prolific arranger in the barbershop style, having had arrangements sung at countless performances and shows and at every level of competition, including on the international stage.

As chair of the Barbershop Harmony Society's Chorus Director Development Committee in its formative years, Biffle helped create the Society's Director Certification Program and the Society's scholarship program for directors attending Harmony University. He is a certified master director and a certified next level trainer.

Throughout his barbershop career, Biffle has continuously coached and taught the art, craft, history, and science of barbershop to individuals, quartets, and choruses all over North America and in England, Wales, the Netherlands, Germany, and Sweden. He has served as faculty and clinician for countless schools, clinics, and festivals and has been on the faculty at the Barbershop Harmony Society's flagship school, Harmony University, numerous times.

During Biffle's eight years on the Society's board of directors, which included two years as president, he chaired the Society Relocation Committee, helping to select Nashville for the Society's new home, purchase a prominent downtown building, and hire an architect and contractor to complete a total remodel for their new headquarters. He is currently concluding a five-year term on the Society Nominating Committee, including two years as chair.

Biffle is in the Halls of Fame of both the Rocky Mountain District and the Albuquerque Chapter of the Barbershop Harmony Society and was the recipient in 1993 of the Darryl Stafford Award for outstanding service to his district. He has served at least once in every administrative position in his home chapter and continues to coach and assist with the music program there.